Becker Professional Education, a global leader in professional education, has been developing study materials for ACCA for more than 20 years, and thousands of candidates studying for the ACCA Qualification have succeeded in their professional examinations through its Platinum and Gold ALP training centers in Central and Eastern Europe and Central Asia.*

Becker Professional Education has also been awarded ACCA Approved Content Provider Status for materials for the Diploma in International Financial Reporting (DipIFR).

Nearly half a million professionals have advanced their careers through Becker Professional Education's courses. Throughout its more than 50-year history, Becker has earned a strong track record of student success through world-class teaching, curriculum and learning tools.

We provide a single destination for individuals and companies in need of global accounting certifications and continuing professional education.

*Platinum – Moscow, Russia and Kiev, Ukraine. Gold – Almaty, Kazakhstan

Becker Professional Education's ACCA Study Materials

All of Becker's materials are authored by experienced ACCA lecturers and are used in the delivery of classroom courses.

Study System: Gives complete coverage of the syllabus with a focus on learning outcomes. It is designed to be used both as part of integrated study. It also includes the ACCA Syllabus and Study Guide, exam advice and commentaries and Bank containing practice questions relating to each topic covered.

Revision Question Bank: Exam style and standard questions together with comprehensive answers to support and prepare exams. The Revision Question Bank also includes past examination questions (updated where relevant), model answers and and tutorial notes.

Revision Essentials*: A condensed, easy-to-use aid to revision containing essential technical content and exam guidance

*Revision Essentials are substantially derived from content reviewed by ACCA's examining team.

Substantially derived from content reviewed by ACCA's examining team

ACCA

PAPER P7

ADVANCED AUDIT AND ASSURANCE (INTERNATIONAL)

REVISION ESSENTIALS
For Examinations to June 2016

No responsibility for loss occasioned to any person acting or refraining from action as a result of any material in this publication can be accepted by the author, editor or publisher.

This training material has been published and prepared by Becker Professional Development International Limited.

16 Elmtree Road
Teddington
TW11 8ST
United Kingdom.

ISBN: 978-1-78566-144-0

Copyright ©2015 DeVry/Becker Educational Development Corp. All rights reserved.

All rights reserved. No part of this training material may be translated, reprinted or reproduced or utilised in any form either in whole or in part or by any electronic, mechanical or other means, now known or hereafter invented, including photocopying and recording, or in any information storage and retrieval system. Request for permission or further information should be addressed to the Permissions Department, DeVry/Becker Educational Development Corp.

For more information about any of Becker's materials, please visit our website at <u>www.becker-atc.com</u> or email <u>acca@becker.com</u>.

CONTENTS

	Page
Syllabus	(iii)
Approach to examining	(iv)
Core topics	(v)
Regulatory environment	0101
Money laundering	0201
Code of ethics for professional accountants	0301
Professional responsibility and liability	0401
Quality control	0501
Professional appointments	0601
Business risk	0701
Planning, material and risk	0801
Evidence	0901
Evaluation and review	1001
Audit of financial statements	1101
Group audits	1201
Assurance services	1301
Reviews and related services	1401
Prospective financial information	1501
Forensic auditing	1601

CONTENTS

	Page
Auditor reports	1701
Additional reading	1801
Examiner's report – June 2015	1901
Analysis of past examinations	2001
Examination technique	2101
Frequently asked questions	2201

CAUTION: These notes offer guidance on key issues. Reliance on these alone is insufficient to pass the examination.

SYLLABUS

Aim

To analyse, evaluate and conclude on the assurance engagement and other audit and assurance issues in the context of best practice and current developments.

Main capabilities

On successful completion of this paper, candidates should be able to:

✓ Recognise the legal and regulatory environment and its impact on audit and assurance practice;

✓ Demonstrate the ability to work effectively on an assurance or other service engagement within a professional and ethical framework;

✓ Assess and recommend appropriate quality control policies and procedures in practice management and recognise the auditor's position in relation to the acceptance and retention of professional appointments;

✓ Identify and formulate the work required to meet the objectives of audit assignments and the apply International Standards on Auditing;

✓ Identify and formulate the work required to meet the objectives of non-audit assignments;

✓ Evaluate findings and the results of work performed and draft suitable reports on assignments; and

✓ Understand the current issues and developments relating to the provision of audit-related and assurance services.

Position within the syllabus

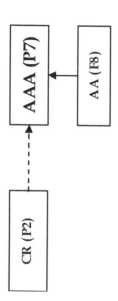

APPROACH TO EXAMINING

Approach to examining the syllabus

The examination is a three hour paper constructed in two sections. Questions in both sections will be largely discursive. However, candidates will be expected, for example, to be able to assess materiality and calculate relevant ratios where applicable.

Section A questions will be based on "case study" type questions. That is not to say that they will be particularly long, rather that they will provide a setting within which a range of topics, issues and requirements can be addressed.

Different types of questions will be encountered in Section B and will tend to be more focused on specific topics, for example "auditor's reports", "quality control" and topics of ISAs which are not examinable in F8, *Audit and Assurance*. (This does not preclude these topics from appearing in Section A). Current issues will be examined across a number of questions.

Time allowed: 3 hours plus 15 minutes reading and planning

Number of marks

Section A:	2 compulsory questions (35 + 25)	60
Section B:	Choice of 2 from 3 (20 marks each)	40
		100

Additional information

Knowledge of new examinable regulations issued by 31st August will be examinable in examination sessions being held in the following calendar year. Documents may be examinable even if the effective date is in the future. This means that all regulations issued by 31st August 2014 will be examinable from the September 2015 to the June 2016 examinations.

The accounting knowledge that is assumed for Paper P7 is the same as that examined in Paper P2. Therefore, candidates studying for Paper P7 should refer to the Accounting Standards issued under Paper P2. Knowledge of exposure drafts and discussion papers within P2 will not be expected.

CORE TOPICS

CORE TOPICS

Tick when completed

Regulatory environment
- ✓ Regulatory framework ☐
- ✓ Money laundering ☐
- ✓ Laws and regulations ☐

Professional and ethical considerations
- ✓ Code of ethics and conduct ☐
- ✓ Fraud and error ☐
- ✓ Professional liability ☐

Practice management
- ✓ Quality control ☐
- ✓ Advertising, publicity, obtaining professional work ☐
- ✓ Tendering ☐
- ✓ Professional appointments ☐

Audit of historical financial information
- ✓ Business risk ☐
- ✓ Planning, materiality, risk ☐
- ✓ Evidence ☐
- ✓ Evaluation and review ☐
- ✓ Group audits ☐

Tick when completed

Other assignments
- ✓ Audit-related and assurance services ☐
- ✓ Review engagements ☐
- ✓ Prospective financial information ☐
- ✓ Forensic audits ☐
- ✓ Internal audit ☐
- ✓ Outsourcing ☐
- ✓ Public sector performance information ☐

Reporting
- ✓ Audit reports ☐
- ✓ Reports to those charged with governance ☐
- ✓ Assurance engagement reports ☐

Current issues and developments
- ✓ Professional and ethical ☐
- ✓ Transnational audits ☐
- ✓ Social, environmental and integrated reporting ☐
- ✓ Auditing standards ☐
- ✓ Accountants, auditors, employers, profession ☐

REGULATORY ENVIRONMENT

1 LAWS, REGULATIONS AND STANDARDS

✓ The assurance profession serves the public interest and has a "social contract" with society.

✓ The structure that audit and assurance services operate under may be summarised as:

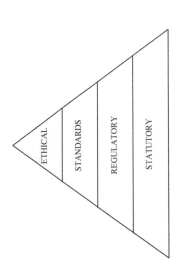

✓ The international regulatory framework for audit and assurance services encompasses:

➢ the pronouncements of the International Federation of Accountants (IFAC); and

➢ principles of corporate governance.

2 STANDARD SETTERS

✓ FATF – the Financial Action Task Force on Money Laundering.

✓ IASB – the International Accounting Standards Board.

✓ IAASB – the International Auditing and Assurance Standards Board.

✓ IESB – the International Ethics Standards Board for Accountants.

✓ IOSCO – the International Organisation of Securities Commissions.

✓ OECD – the Organisation for Economic Cooperation and Development.

3 PUBLIC INTEREST OVERSIGHT BOARDS

3.1 Public interest

✓ The collective well-being of the community of people and institutions the professional accountant serves.

3.2 Bodies

IFAC

✓ Oversees IFAC's auditing and assurance, ethics, and education standard-setting activities as well as its Member Body Compliance Program.

REGULATORY ENVIRONMENT

US – Sarbanes-Oxley (SoX)

✓ The Public Company Accounting Oversight Board (PCAOB) created to protect investors and the public interest by promoting informative, fair, and independent audit reports.

UK – Audit Regulations

✓ Areas covered by the Regulations include:

- Eligibility/application to become a registered auditor;
- Qualifications (entry requirements, training, post-qualification experience);
- Conduct of audit work (application of auditing standards);
- Compliance and monitoring (application of the Regulations and reviews);
- Regulatory action; and
- Disciplinary procedures.

UK – Financial Reporting Council (FRC)

✓ UK's independent regulator responsible for promoting high quality corporate governance and reporting to foster investment:

- Promotes high standards of corporate governance through the UK Corporate Governance Code and UK Stewardship Code;
- Sets the professional standards for corporate reporting, auditing and actuarial practice;
- Monitors and enforces accounting, auditing and ethical standards;
- Oversees the regulatory activities of the actuarial profession and the professional accountancy bodies; and
- Operates independent disciplinary arrangements for public interest cases involving accountants, auditors and actuaries.

REGULATORY ENVIRONMENT

4 AUDIT COMMITTEES

4.1 UK Corporate Governance Code

Controls and systems

- ✓ Integrity of the financial statements.
- ✓ Internal controls and risk management systems.
- ✓ Annual report is fair, balanced and understandable.
- ✓ "Whistle-blowing" procedures.
- ✓ Annual report allows users to assess company's performance, business model and strategy.

Internal audit

- ✓ Effectiveness of internal audit.
- ✓ Asses work plan and findings.
- ✓ Monitor management's responsiveness to findings.
- ✓ Appointment/termination of head of internal audit.
- ✓ Direct access to board chairman/Audit Committee and accountable to the Audit Committee.

External audit

- ✓ Appointment, re-appointment and removal.
- ✓ Remuneration and terms of engagement.
- ✓ Independence and effectiveness of audit process.
- ✓ Engagement to supply non-audit services.
- ✓ Results of audit process, representation letter, management letter.

4.2 Advantages and disadvantages

Advantages

- ✓ High level, effective and informed oversight.
- ✓ Enhances market, public and stakeholder confidence.
- ✓ Composed of independent NEDs using own initiative.
- ✓ Link for internal/external auditors to NEDs.
- ✓ Deterrent to fraud.

Disadvantages

- ✗ Seen as an unnecessary legal/regulatory burden.
- ✗ Additional cost (not cost effective).
- ✗ Difficulty in finding appropriate NEDs.
- ✗ Risks and burdens of responsibility for NEDs.
- ✗ May not be able to embed (in systems and culture).

MONEY LAUNDERING

1 BACKGROUND

1.1 Money laundering

The process by which criminals attempt to conceal the true origin and ownership of the proceeds of criminal activity allowing them to maintain control over the proceeds and, ultimately, providing a legitimate cover for illegal income.

1.2 FATF

✓ The Financial Action Task Force on Money Laundering is an inter-governmental body which sets standards, and develops and promotes policies to combat money laundering and terrorist financing.

Policies

✓ Legal systems including scope of the criminal offence.

✓ Measures to be taken by financial institutions and non-financial businesses and professions to prevent money laundering and terrorist financing:

  ▸ customer due diligence (CDD) and record-keeping;
  ▸ reporting suspicious transactions and compliance to an external financial intelligence unit (FIU).

✓ Transparency of legal persons and arrangements.

✓ International co-operation including mutual legal assistance and extradition.

2 OFFENCES AND PENALTIES (UK)

2.1 Principal offences

✓ Failure to appoint a Money Laundering Reporting Officer (MLRO).

✓ Failure to implement appropriate risk management procedures and internal controls to comply with anti-money laundering legislation.

✓ Failure to undertake verification of identity of all new clients before commencing a business relationship.

✓ Failure to apply ongoing monitoring of business relationships, client due diligence and transactions.

✓ Obtaining, concealing, retaining or investing funds or property or providing assistance to another to do so, if professional accountants know or suspect that those funds or property are the proceeds of crime.

✓ Failure to report any knowledge or suspicion as soon as practicable that money laundering activities are being carried out ("a suspicion report").

✓ Failure to report a belief or suspicion of terrorist money laundering in the course of their trade or profession.

✓ Doing or disclosing anything that might prejudice an investigation into such activities (e.g. "tipping off").

0201

MONEY LAUNDERING

- Proceeding with a transaction without the consent of the relevant authority following the submission of a suspicion report.
- Falsifying, concealing or destroying documents relevant to a money laundering investigation.
- Failure to comply with a direction of the relevant authority not to proceed with a transaction or business relationship.
- Failure to maintain records in accordance with legislative requirements.

2.2 Fiscal offences

- Tax evasion.

2.3 Knowledge or suspicion

- Knowledge is likely to include
  - actual knowledge;
  - shutting one's mind to the obvious;
  - refraining from making inquiries;
  - deterring a person from making disclosures; and
  - knowledge of circumstances which would indicate the facts to an honest and reasonable person and failing to make reasonable inquiries which such a person would have made.

2.4 Tipping-off

- When an individual who has knowledge or suspicion makes a disclosure to a third party (e.g. the suspected individual or entity) which is likely to prejudice a terrorist or money laundering investigation.
- Non-disclosure and non-action may be effective tipping off (e.g. not carrying out a client's instructions that would be money laundering may be sufficient to put them on guard).

2.5 Professional duty of confidence

- Accounting professionals (e.g. ACCA members) will not be in breach of any professional duty of confidence if they report, in good faith, any money laundering knowledge or suspicions to the appropriate authority.

MONEY LAUNDERING

3 PREVENTATIVE MEASURES

3.1 Risk management, internal controls and policies

- Establishing a top-down, risk-based, anti-money laundering culture in the organisation.

- Identifying money laundering and terrorist financing risks relevant to the professional accountant's business:
  - Being used by clients to launder assets;
  - Products and services offered that could aid money laundering;
  - Client types and sectors, jurisdictions of client origin, funding and investment; and
  - Client activities, reputation, contacts and public profile.

- Designing and implementing controls to manage and mitigate these risks, and record their operation.

- Ensure that anyone who suspects money laundering knows how to report this information to the MLRO.

- Provide the MLRO with the means by which the reasonableness of the suspicion can be judged to assess which suspicions should be reported.

- Client acceptance procedures;
  - identification procedures; and
  - "know your client" ("KYC") information (e.g. expected patterns of business, business model and source of funds).

- Client money procedures should include KYC, commercial purpose of the transaction, source and destination of the funds.

3.2 MLRO

- Should have a suitable level of seniority and experience (e.g. a principal of an accountancy firm).

Responsibilities

- Considering internal reports of money laundering.
- Deciding if there are sufficient grounds for suspicion.
- Preparing external reports for the appropriate authority.
- Advising the engagement individual/team how to continue their work and interact with the client.
- Training the firm's employees in anti-money laundering and reporting suspicion procedures.
- Advising on how to guard against risks of tipping off or prejudicing an investigation.
- Designing and implementing internal anti-money laundering systems and procedures.

3.3 Record keeping

- All client identification records and records of all transactions, with a full audit trail, must be maintained.
- Records of transactions must be kept in a readily retrievable form for a period of at least 5 years.

3.4 Client due diligence

- Client due diligence measures need to be carried out:
  - when establishing a business relationship;
  - when carrying out an occasional transaction;
  - where there is a suspicion of money laundering; and
  - where there are doubts concerning the accuracy and reliability of previous identification information.

- Sufficient information must be obtained, before any potential client can be accepted, to understand:
  - who the client is;
  - for an entity, who owns (and ultimately owns) it;
  - who controls it;
  - the purpose and intended nature of the business relationship;
  - the nature of the client;
  - the client's sources of funds; and
  - the client's business and economic purpose.

- For a normal risk individual, typical documentation includes official items, with a photograph, establishing the client's full name and permanent address.
- For a normal risk entity, obtaining certificate of incorporation, company's registered address and a list of shareholders and directors.
- Check detail against lists of known terrorist, terrorist organisations and other sanctions information.
- The greater the risk, the greater the depth, strength and detail of KYC.

3.5 Suspicion

Recognition

- It is impossible to define suspicion.
- A suspicious transaction/situation will often be inconsistent with the client's known legitimate business or personal activities. Hence, KYC.

Examples of potentially suspicious transactions

- Unusually large cash deposits.
- Frequent exchange of cash into other currencies.
- A transaction where the counter-party is unknown;
- Any activity inconsistent with normal business activity.

MONEY LAUNDERING

- ✓ Any activity involving off-shore business arrangements where no clear business purpose underlies them.

Reporting

- ✓ Professional accountants are legally required to report knowledge or suspicions of money laundering to the appropriate authority.

- ✓ It is a criminal offence not to do so.

- ✓ There are no "de minimis" concessions. The obligation to report is irrespective of the amount involved or the seriousness of the offence.

3.6 Educating and training all staff

- ✓ Relevant individuals must be provided with training on:
  - ▲ how to report to the MLRO;
  - ▲ how to identify clients;
  - ▲ how to recognise and deal with money laundering situations;
  - ▲ the main money laundering offences; and
  - ▲ procedures to forestall and prevent money laundering, including identification, record keeping and reporting procedures.

4 "PROFESSIONAL CLEARANCE" LETTERS

- ✓ If suspicion has been (or may be) reported, businesses and individuals need to be cautious in responding to "professional clearance" letters.

- ✓ It is recommended that businesses and individuals do not respond to questions in professional clearance letters concerning either:
  - ▲ their satisfaction as to the identity of an entity or individual; or
  - ▲ whether any report of suspicion has been made, or contemplated.

5 ANTI-MONEY LAUNDERING PROGRAMME

5.1 Basic elements

- ✓ Dedicated resources.
- ✓ Written policies and procedures.
- ✓ Comprehensive coverage.
- ✓ Timely escalation and resolution of matters.
- ✓ Explicit management support.
- ✓ Sufficient training and education.
- ✓ Regular review/audit of the program.

CODE OF ETHICS FOR PROFESSIONAL ACCOUNTANTS

1 PROFESSIONAL CODES

1.1 Purpose

- ✓ To provide professional accountants with guidelines for maintaining an appropriate attitude and enhancing the accountancy profession.
- ✓ To give accountability to the public.
- ✓ To codify behaviour beyond that which is incorporated in legislation.

1.2 IESBA Code of Ethics for Professional Accountants

- ✓ A committee of IFAC, the International Ethics Standards Board of Accountants prepares and issues the *Code of Ethics for Professional Accountants*.
- ✓ It is intended to serve as a model for the member bodies of IFAC.
- ✓ It sets standards of conduct and states fundamental principles to be the basis on which the minimum ethical requirements should be founded.

2 ACCA CODE OF ETHICS AND CONDUCT

- ✓ Derived from the IESBA code.

2.1 Fundamental principles

- ✓ Integrity.
- ✓ Objectivity.
- ✓ Professional competence and due care.
- ✓ Confidentiality.
- ✓ Professional behaviour.

2.2 Conceptual Framework

Assists professional accountants (through guidance and illustrative examples) in identifying, evaluating and responding to threats to compliance with the fundamental principles, rather than merely following rules).

2.3 Threats

- ✓ Self-interest.
- ✓ Self-review.
- ✓ Advocacy.
- ✓ Familiarity.
- ✓ Intimidation.

CODE OF ETHICS FOR PROFESSIONAL ACCOUNTANTS

2.4 Safeguards

- Aim to eliminate or reduce to an acceptable level the threats faced.
- Will vary depending on the circumstances.

Two types

- Created by the profession, legislation or regulation.
- Within the work environment.

2.5 Ethical conflict resolution

- Relevant facts.
- Ethical issues involved.
- Fundamental principles involved.
- Established procedures followed.
- The action followed and outcome.
- Alternative courses of action and consequences.
- Internal and external sources of consultation.

3 INTEGRITY, OBJECTIVITY AND INDEPENDENCE

3.1 Principles and threats

- Integrity and objectivity must be beyond question.
- Independence in mind **and** independence in appearance.

Threats to integrity and objectivity

- Fees and pricing (self-interest, intimidation).
- Overdue fees (self-interest).
- Actual or threatened litigation (self-interest, intimidation).
- Family and other personal relationships (self-interest, familiarity, intimidation).
- Close business relationships (self-interest, intimidation).
- Financial interests (self-interest):
  - Partners.
  - Employees.
  - Close family member.
- Loans and guarantees (self-interest).
- Gifts and hospitality (self-interest, familiarity).

CODE OF ETHICS FOR PROFESSIONAL ACCOUNTANTS

- Provision of other services:
  - Preparing accounting records/financial statements (self-review).
  - Valuation services (self-review).
  - Internal audit (self-review).
  - IT systems services (self-review).
  - Provision of temporary staff self-review).
  - Provision of litigation support services (self-review, advocacy).
  - Provision of legal services (self-review, advocacy).
  - Recruitment of senior management (self-interest, familiarity, intimidation).
  - Corporate financial services (advocacy, self-review).
- Long association (self-interest, familiarity).
- Recent employment with an assurance client (self-interest, self-review, familiarity).
- Future employment with an assurance client (familiarity, intimidation, self-interest).
- Serving on the board of an assurance client (self-interest, self-review).
- Second opinions (professional competence, due care).

4 CONFIDENTIALITY

4.1 Improper disclosure

- Information acquired in the course of professional work should not be disclosed to third parties.

Exceptions

- With client's permission.
- Disclosure is **obligatory** required (no need for permission) by a legal, regulatory or professional duty.
- Disclosure is made (voluntarily) "in the public interest" (auditor's right to disclose).

4.2 Improper use

- Information acquired in the course of professional work should not be used (or appear to be used) for personal advantage.
  - Also applies to advantage of a third party.
- Experience gained can be used in another employment.
- Proprietary procedures and systems cannot.

CODE OF ETHICS FOR PROFESSIONAL ACCOUNTANTS

5 CONFLICTS OF INTEREST

5.1 Professional accountant v client

- ✓ Should place clients' interests before own interests.
- ✓ Should not accept or continue an engagement if there is or is likely to be a *significant* conflict of interests.
- ✓ Any financial gain in excess of normal fees will always result in a significant conflict.

5.2 Client v client

- ✓ Avoid the interests of one client adversely affecting those of another.
- ✓ Material conflicts should be sufficiently disclosed to enable all parties to make an informed decision whether to engage or continue their relationship with the firm.
- ✓ If necessary, decline acceptance or discontinue.

Safeguards

- ✓ Strict policies, training and disciplinary actions.
- ✓ Different assignment teams and regular independent review.
- ✓ Confidentiality agreements.
- ✓ Advising clients to seek independent legal advice.
- ✓ Disengagement as quickly as client's interests allow if threat cannot be reduced to an acceptable level.

6 ADVERTISING

- ✓ Must not bring the profession into disrepute when marketing professional services.
- ✓ Must be honest and truthful and not make:
  - ▲ exaggerated claims for services offered, qualifications possessed, or experience gained; or
  - ▲ disparaging remarks or unsubstantiated comparisons to the work of another.

6.1 Advertising

- ✓ May contain any factual statement the truth of which can be justified (but not unflattering to others).
- ✓ Must not:
  - ✗ bring ACCA into disrepute or discredit accountants, firms or the profession;
  - ✗ discredit the services offered by other professional accountants;
  - ✗ claim superiority;
  - ✗ mislead (directly or by implication); or
  - ✗ fall short of local and national regulatory standards regarding legality, decency, clarity, honesty and truthfulness.

CODE OF ETHICS FOR PROFESSIONAL ACCOUNTANTS

7 FEES

7.1 Basis of fees

- General basis on which fees are computed should be set out in:
  - promotional material;
  - tender documents; and
  - the letter of engagement.

- Professional accountants can charge whatever fee they consider appropriate based on:
  - Seniority and professional expertise of persons engaged in work;
  - Time taken;
  - Risk and responsibility entailed in work;
  - Urgency and importance of work to client; and
  - Overhead expenses.

- Fees must not be calculated for an assurance engagement on a percentage or contingency basis.

7.2 Fee quotations

- A firm may obtain an assurance engagement for a fee level that is significantly lower than that charged by the predecessor firm, or quoted by another firm.
- The firm must be able to demonstrate that:
  - the client has not been misled;
  - appropriate time and qualified staff are assigned to the task; and
  - all applicable assurance standards, guidelines and quality control procedures are being complied with.

8 DESCRIPTIONS AND NAMES.

- Chartered Certified Accountant(s) cannot be used as part of the registered name.
- Should be consistent with the dignity of the profession.
- May indicate the range of services offered
- Should not be misleading.
- Should not be objectionable.

PROFESSIONAL RESPONSIBILITY AND LIABILITY

1 FRAUD AND ERROR (ISA 240)

Objectives

- ✓ To identify and assess risks of material misstatement.
- ✓ To obtain sufficient appropriate audit evidence.
- ✓ To respond appropriately to fraud or suspected fraud.

1.1 Definitions

Fraud – *intentional* act involving deception to obtain an unjust or illegal advantage.

Fraud risk factors – events or conditions indicating an incentive, pressure or opportunity to commit fraud.

Error – *unintentional* mistake in the financial statements (including omission).

1.2 Types of fraud

Fraudulent financial reporting

- ✓ Misstatements or omissions intended to deceive users:
  - ➤ Accounting records or supporting documents;
  - ➤ Events, transactions balances or other information;
  - ➤ Measurement, recognition and disclosure.

Misappropriation of assets

- ✓ Theft or misuse (both tangible and intangible).

1.3 Management and auditor responsibilities

Those charged with governance and management

- ✓ To prevent and detect fraud and error:
  - ➤ Emphasis on prevention and risk management;
  - ➤ Ensure culture of honesty and ethical behaviour.

Auditor

- ✓ To obtain reasonable assurance that financial statements are free from *material* misstatement (fraud or error):
  - ➤ Critical application of professional scepticism;
  - ➤ Consider susceptibility of misstatement due to fraud.
- ✓ Is **not** responsible for prevention of fraud and error.

1.4 Risk assessment procedures

- ✓ Discussions with the engagement team (for example):
  - ➤ how and where the financial statements may be susceptible to material misstatement due to fraud;
  - ➤ how management could perpetrate and conceal fraudulent financial reporting;
  - ➤ how assets could be misappropriated;
  - ➤ circumstances that might indicate aggressive earnings management;

PROFESSIONAL RESPONSIBILITY AND LIABILITY

- management practices that could lead to fraudulent financial reporting;
- unusual/unexplained changes in behaviour/lifestyle of management or employees;
- types of circumstances relevant to the client that, if met, might indicate the possibility of fraud;
- how unpredictability will be incorporated into the nature, timing and extent of audit procedures;
- audit procedures to be selected to respond to the entity's susceptibility to fraud; and
- the risk of management override of controls.

✓ Fraud control design, implementation and effectiveness.

✓ Inquiries (to identify incentives, opportunity, etc) of:
- those charged with governance;
- risk management personnel;
- internal audit;
- direct and indirect operating personnel;
- employees who deal with susceptible transactions;
- internal and external legal services.

✓ Revenue is always a significant fraud risk. If considered not to be, full explanations must be documented.

1.5 Effect on audit strategy and extent of work

Audit strategy

- ✓ Increase professional scepticism.
- ✓ Reassess audit approach.
- ✓ Nature, timing and extent of substantive procedures.
- ✓ Procedures to match the risks identified.

Audit team

- ✓ Specialist skills.
- ✓ Stronger briefing, supervision and review.
- ✓ Higher level of experienced staff.

Extent of audit procedures

- ✓ Should not be predictable.
- ✓ Use of experts.
- ✓ Physical inspection of "at risk" assets.
- ✓ Targeted CAATs, data-mining, benchmarking.
- ✓ Targeted analytical procedures.
- ✓ Specific confirmation requests.
- ✓ Post prior-year audit transactions.

Override of controls

- ✓ Journal entries and other adjustments.
- ✓ Accounting estimates.
- ✓ Business transaction rationale.
- ✓ Transactions outside of normal procedures.

PROFESSIONAL RESPONSIBILITY AND LIABILITY

1.6 Evaluation of audit evidence

- ✓ Errors indicative of fraud.
- ✓ Nature and cumulative effect of errors.
- ✓ Discrepancies in the accounting records.
- ✓ Conflicting or missing evidence.
- ✓ Declining auditor-client relationship.

1.7 Written representations

- ✓ Management's responsibility for design, implementation and maintenance of internal control to prevent and detect fraud.
- ✓ Disclosure to the auditor of:
  - ▲ the results of management's risk assessment; and
  - ▲ knowledge of fraud or suspected fraud.

1.8 Communication with management and those charged with governance

- ✓ If there is doubt on whom to report, auditors must seek legal advice, or ACCA advice, before taking any action.

Management

- ✓ Factual findings.
- ✓ Timely (if verbal, follow up in writing).
- ✓ Report to management level above those implicated.

Those charged with governance

- ✓ Communicate all actual, suspicions of, or weaknesses in controls relating to, fraud.
- ✓ Communicate concerns (if any) about management's attitude to managing fraud risk.
- ✓ Discuss (e.g. with the audit committee) any implications for further audit procedures.

Regulatory and enforcement authorities

- ✓ Duty of confidentiality normally precludes.
- ✓ If duty can be overridden, seek legal advice.
- ✓ May be statutory duty without informing the client.

1.9 Withdrawal from the engagement

- ✓ In exceptional circumstances:
  - ▲ Management does not take the necessary remedial action regarding fraud;
  - ▲ Results of audit tests indicate a significant risk of material and pervasive fraud; and/or
  - ▲ There are significant doubts about the competence or integrity of management (or those charged with governance).

PROFESSIONAL RESPONSIBILITY AND LIABILITY

Factors to consider

- Whether management or those charged with governance are implicated.
- The effects on the auditor of continuing an association with the client.
- Any professional and legal responsibilities in such circumstances.
- The alternatives, if any, to withdrawal.
- Legal advice.

2 LAWS AND REGULATIONS

2.1 Non-compliance

- Acts of omission or commission (intentional or unintentional) by an entity or on behalf of the entity, that are contrary to prevailing laws or regulations.

2.2 Types of laws and regulations

- Direct – affect form and content of the financial statements (e.g. IFRS, true & fair view).
- Indirect – affect operational aspects or conduct of the business that may impact the financial statements (e.g. operating licence, breaches of health & safety laws, financial consequences).

2.3 Management and auditor responsibilities

- Management – to ensure that operations are conducted within the laws and regulations applicable to the entity.
  - Control environment and systems.
- Auditors – to plan, perform and evaluate the audit recognising material effects of non-compliance.
  - Procedures are similar to audit approach to fraud.

2.4 Indications that non-compliance may have occurred

- Enquiries or investigations by regulators, authorities, etc.
- Fines and penalties.
- Indications of fraud.
- Media comment.

2.5 Non-compliance discovered

Considerations

- Nature, circumstances, effect on financial statements.
- Potential consequences include:
  - fines/penalties;
  - damages;
  - threat of expropriation of assets;
  - enforced discontinuation of operations; or
  - litigation.
- Implications for the audit report.

0404

©2015 DeVry/Becker Educational Development Corp. All rights reserved.

2.6 Reporting non-compliance and withdrawal from engagement

✓ Essentially the same as for fraud and error.

3 EXPECTATIONS GAP

✓ The difference between what the public believes the auditor ought to do and report and what the audit profession requires its members to do and report.

✓ Public view – fraud prevention should be part of the auditor's work ("where were the auditors?")

✓ Auditor's view – to plan and perform the audit taking into consideration (reasonable assurance) the risk of material misstatement arising from fraud and error.

3.1 Components

✓ Reporting gap – the profession's and public's view of what should be reported differ.

✓ Performance gap – where auditors perform below existing standards.

✓ Liability gap – the profession's and public's view of to whom the auditor is liable are different.

3.2 Bridging the gap

Detection of fraud

✓ Auditors should detect fraud – requires fundamental change in the nature and objective of the audit.

✓ Regular forensic audit for all public interest entities should be introduced.

Independent oversight

✓ IFAC, FRC and SoX have established public oversight bodies and independent standard setting, monitoring and disciplinary bodies.

Audit report

✓ Must be more informative to enable users to make relevant/reliable investment and fiduciary decisions.

✓ Updated audit report ISAs issued in January 2015. Effective for audits of financial statements for periods ending on or after December 15, 2016.

4 LIABILITY

4.1 In contract

✓ The auditor has a contractual relationship with his client – and may therefore be sued for breach of contract.

✓ The auditor must carry out his work with "reasonable skill and care". Failure to do so is a negligent breach of contract.

✓ Negligence is determined through:

- ▲ A duty of care was owed;
- ▲ A breach of that duty has arisen; and
- ▲ Financial loss has been suffered.

✓ A duty of care would be owed where:

- ▲ Foreseeability of damage to the third party;
- ▲ A relationship of "proximity" with the third party; and
- ▲ A situation where it would be fair, just and reasonable to impose a duty of a given scope on the professional accountants.

4.2 Limiting liability

✓ In general, auditors are prohibited by many jurisdictions from entering into arrangements to limit their liability.

✓ In some jurisdictions liability may be limited through:

- ▲ Limited liability partnerships (LLP);
- ▲ liability limitation agreements.

✓ Arguments for, include:

- ▲ joint and several liability is unfair where other parties (e.g. directors) may also share negligence;
- ▲ the audit market may shrink as a leading firm may be sued out of existence;
- ▲ higher risk entities (e.g. international organisations) may become un-auditable; and
- ▲ fees may substantially increase to cover higher risks.

Limited liability partnerships

✓ Separate legal entity is liable to the full extent of its assets.

✓ Liability of LLP members is limited to their investment.

✓ Personal assets of each member are protected.

✓ Negligent engagement partners can be individually sued.

✓ LLPs are required to file audited annual financial statements.

PROFESSIONAL RESPONSIBILITY AND LIABILITY

Limited liability agreements

- Permit companies to limit the liability of their auditors provided that shareholder approval is obtained.
- Not the same as a disclaimer of responsibility in the audit report.
- To be valid the agreement must:
  - be fair and reasonable in the circumstances;
  - be for the current year only; and
  - approved by a resolution of the entity's shareholders.
- The contractual limits could be set on:
  - the auditor's proportional share of the responsibility for any loss;
  - a monetary cap;
  - an agreed formula (e.g. x times the audit fee); or
  - the "fair and reasonable" test.

5 LITIGATION

5.1 Managing

- Sound client acceptance procedures.
- Engagement letters.
- Quality control.
- Full documentation and notes.
- Using expert advice.
- Clauses disclaiming liability to third parties (e.g. Bannerman clause).
- Limiting use of reports.
- Hold harmless clauses.
- Professional indemnity insurance (PII).

QUALITY CONTROL

1 QUALITY CONTROLS

1.1 Documents

- ✓ Statements of Membership Obligations – SMO 1 *Quality Assurance Implemented by Member Bodies.*
- ✓ International Standard on Quality Control – ISQC 1.
- ✓ International Standard on Auditing – ISA 220.
- ✓ Audit Quality Framework.

1.2 Importance of quality control

- ✓ Achieve audit objectives.
- ✓ Operate effectively, efficiently and economically.
- ✓ Avoid disputes with clients
- ✓ Minimise risk of litigation.
- ✓ Provide a professional service to clients.
- ✓ Ensure regulatory body visits proceed smoothly.
- ✓ Ensure staff are monitored and controlled.
- ✓ Help identify training needs at all levels.
- ✓ Ensure staff appraisal systems operate effectively at all levels.

2 AUDIT FIRM – ISQC 1

2.1 Elements

- ✓ Leadership responsibilities for quality within the firm – "the buck stops here".
- ✓ Ethical requirements – Code of Ethics, staff declarations, identify and deal with threats to independence, senior staff rotation.
- ✓ Acceptance and continuance of client relationships and specific engagements.
- ✓ Human resources – recruitment, training, career development, performance reviews, technical standards, professional competence, commitment to ethical, legal and regulatory standards.
- ✓ Assignment of engagement teams.
- ✓ Engagement performance – briefing, supervision, review.
- ✓ Consultation – internal and external with experts (e.g. to resolve difficult or contentious issues).
- ✓ Engagement quality control review – pre-issuance (hot") reviews of all listed/high risk assignments.
- ✓ Monitoring – reasonable assurance that quality control works (e.g. post issuance ("cold") reviews).

QUALITY CONTROL

3 INDIVIDUAL AUDIT

3.1 ISA 220

✓ Applies ISQC 1 requirements to the level of the individual audit.

- Engagement partner takes leadership responsibilities.
- Firm and audit staff are independent of client and have complied with all ethical requirements.
- Acceptance review carried out (e.g. integrity of client, ability to act, engagement letter).
- Engagement team has appropriate abilities and competence.
- Appropriate direction, supervision and review planned and applied.
- Sufficient appropriate audit evidence obtained to support the audit opinion.
- Consultation undertaken, correctly applied and recorded.
- Engagement review planned and actioned.

3.2 Assignment of engagement teams

✓ Understanding and practical experience (as a whole) of:

- audit procedures;
- professional standards;
- regulatory and legal requirements;
- technical knowledge;
- professional judgement and scepticism; and
- quality control procedures.

3.3 Direction

✓ Informing engagement team of:

- their responsibilities;
- nature of the business;
- risk-related issues; and
- detailed audit approach.

✓ May be communicated through:

- team briefing (face to face)
- audit programme;
- time budgets; and
- overall audit strategy and plan (planning memoranda).

3.4 Supervision

✓ The monitoring of the assignment progress to consider whether:

- assistants have the necessary skills and competence;
- assistants understand the audit directions; and
- work is being carried out in accordance with the overall audit plan and the audit program.

✓ Informed of and addresses significant accounting and auditing questions.

✓ Resolves any differences of professional judgment between personnel.

✓ Identify matters requiring higher level consultation.

3.5 Review

✓ Work performed by each assistant needs to be reviewed by more experienced personnel to consider:

- work performed is in accordance with audit program;
- work performed and results obtained are adequately documented;
- all significant audit matters have been resolved or are reflected in audit conclusions;
- objectives of audit procedures have been achieved;
- audit evidence is sufficient and appropriate to support audit opinion; and
- conclusions expressed are consistent with the results of the work performed and support the audit opinion.

3.6 Quality control review formats

✓ Audit review panel.
✓ Second partner review.
✓ Pre-issuance (hot) review.
✓ Post-issuance (cold) review.

QUALITY CONTROL

4 AUDIT QUALITY FRAMEWORK

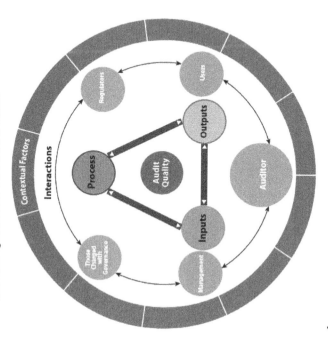

Inputs

- ✓ Auditors':
  - ➢ values, ethics, attitudes; and
  - ➢ knowledge, skills, experience.

Process

- ✓ Rigorous audit process and quality control.

Outputs

- ✓ External (e.g. audit report) and internal (e.g. deficiencies letter).

Interactions

- ✓ Key players in the financial supply chain.
  - ➢ Auditors, management, those charged with governance, shareholders, regulators, users.

Contextual

- ✓ Factors that have the potential to affect the nature and quality of financial reporting and audit quality.
  - ➢ Reporting framework.
  - ➢ Laws and regulations.
  - ➢ Business practices.
  - ➢ Corporate governance.
  - ➢ Culture.
  - ➢ Litigation environment.
  - ➢ Audit regulation.
  - ➢ Human resources.

PROFESSIONAL APPOINTMENTS

1 NEW APPOINTMENTS

1.1 Professional scepticism

- Throughout the entire client screening, professional enquiry and engagement acceptance procedure, it is critical that the auditor applies professional scepticism.

Situations

- The reason for changing auditor.
- Reasons for disagreements with previous auditor.
- Understanding the integrity of those charged with governance and management.
- Establishing pre-conditions of an audit.
- Understanding the entity and its business environment.
- Understanding the control environment.
- Application of accounting policies, use of estimation and fair values.
- Use of management's experts.
- Areas that require a high degree of subjectivity.
- Assessing responses to professional enquiries.

2 CLIENT SCREENING AND ACCEPTANCE

- A quality control (due diligence) procedure to ensure appropriate ethical and business considerations are undertaken before a new client is accepted/current appointment continued and the associated risks assessed.

  - Ability to audit (potential) client – practical and ethical considerations.
  - Understanding the business – governance, environment, risks, processes, controls.
  - Association with the (potential) client – reputational risk.
  - Financial viability of the (potential) client – fee recovery.
  - Legal requirements – money laundering "due diligence".
  - Logistics – timing, staff allocation, specialist requirements.

- Question – "Do we wish to accept/continue with this firm as a client?"

PROFESSIONAL APPOINTMENTS

3 PROFESSIONAL ENQUIRY

3.1 Nominee

- An accountant who is asked to accept appointment should:
  - ➤ request prospective client's permission to communicate with existing accountant; and
  - ➤ with permission, write to existing accountant requesting information relevant to deciding whether or not to accept the appointment.
- If permission is refused, the appointment must be declined.
- If a conflicting view between client and current auditor/adviser is raised, discuss with client to be satisfied that:
  - ➤ client's view can be accepted as reasonable; and/or
  - ➤ client will accept that nominee might express a contrary opinion.
- If current auditor/adviser does not respond within a reasonable time:
  - ➤ phone or fax; and
  - ➤ if all else fails, send a final letter by recorded means stating that "no matters" will be assumed unless advised otherwise.

3.2 Existing accountant

- Should obtain client's permission to discuss his affairs with prospective accountant.
- They should answer without delay:
  - ➤ that there are no matters that the prospective accountant should be aware of; or
  - ➤ factors that the prospective accountant should be aware of.
- Existence of unpaid fees is not of itself a reason for declining nomination.

3.3 Working papers

- Access to working papers assists successor auditor's work (e.g. on opening balances and comparatives.
- Client and nominee auditor usually have no rights of access to existing auditor's working papers.
- Professional courtesy may permit reasonable access to key working papers.
- In some jurisdictions (e.g. UK) it is a legal requirement to allow access to working papers.
  - ➤ Proprietary documents and audit methodology cannot be accessed.

4 TERMS OF AUDIT ENGAGEMENT

4.1 Preconditions

To establish if the preconditions for an audit are present, the auditor should:

- ✓ Assess the appropriateness and acceptability of the financial reporting framework;
- ✓ Obtain management's agreement that it acknowledges and understands its responsibilities for:
  - the preparation and fair presentation of the financial statements (according to the framework);
  - internal controls (so financial statements are free from material misstatement); and
  - providing the auditor with unrestricted access to all relevant information and necessary persons (to obtain audit evidence).

4.2 Purpose of the engagement letter

- ✓ Helps avoid misunderstanding between client and auditor.
- ✓ Documents and confirms:
  - acceptance of respective responsibilities;
  - auditor's acceptance of the appointment;
  - the applicable reporting framework;
  - objective and scope of the work (audit); and
  - form and content of reports (including modifications, limitations and restrictions on use).
- ✓ May have a separate section dealing with other relevant details (e.g. fees, timetable, other services, etc).
- ✓ Should be reviewed at time of re-acceptance of assignment and new letter issued for changes in legislation/GAAP, new directors etc.

PROFESSIONAL APPOINTMENTS

Main contents

- ✓ Objective and scope of the audit.
- ✓ Management's responsibilities.
- ✓ Financial reporting framework applied.
- ✓ The form of the audit report.
- ✓ The fact that some material misstatement may remain undiscovered.
  - ▸ Expectation of receiving written management representations.
  - ▸ Unrestricted access to records, documentation, etc.
  - ▸ Agreement that management will inform the auditors of any material subsequent events.
  - ▸ Basis on which fees are computed and any billing arrangements.

5 TENDERING

- ✓ The process of inviting more than one firm to compete for the assurance assignment of the enterprise.

5.1 Potential benefits

For the enterprise

- ✓ Obtaining the service at a lower cost or a better service for the same cost or improved service content at a competitive cost.
- ✓ Being able to compare firms' methodologies, services and cultures.
- ✓ Being able to establish the "best fit" with a firm.

For the audit firm appointed

- ✓ A new (good) client and fee obtained, on the basis of successful client screening procedures.
- ✓ Knowledge obtained during the tendering process will assist in an effective first audit.
- ✓ Knowledge and experience gained may have application to current clients, future clients and future tenders.

5.2 Potential risks

For the enterprise

- ✗ Being "blinded by the presentation" and failing to identify the true (negative) features of the firm or failing to identify the intangible benefits of the firm.
- ✗ Being "low balled" and failing to appreciate the true costs of additional services or the potential increases in service fees in future years.

For the audit firm appointed

- ✗ Inability to recover the tender costs plus a substantial reduction in audit fees – the level of audit work cannot be compromised.
- ✗ Poor client screening may result in accepting a "rogue" client – risk of damage to the firm's reputation.

5.3 Tendering process (enterprise)

- ✓ Shortlist firms – reputation, recommendation, experience.
- ✓ Prepare and send invitation to tender.
- ✓ Provide necessary information to firms as requested.
- ✓ Evaluate documentary submissions and select for presentation stage.
- ✓ Oral presentations and Q&A sessions.
- ✓ Notification of decision.

5.4 Invitation to tender

- ✓ Need to give a broad indication of the information required to be included in the audit firm's written responses.

    - ▲ Background on firm;
    - ▲ Experience of firm in the relevant sector;
    - ▲ Audit team (e.g. biographies);
    - ▲ Range of services;
    - ▲ Approach to the audit; and
    - ▲ Fees.

- ✓ Some general background to the organisation's activities (e.g. an annual report) may be enclosed with the invitation.

PROFESSIONAL APPOINTMENTS

5.5 To bid, or not to bid

Matters to be considered

- ✓ Technical proficiency of the firm to carry out the audit.
- ✓ Worth investing in a new sector and keeping up to date.
- ✓ Geographical and international aspects.
- ✓ Other commitments to existing client base.
- ✓ Staffing arrangements.
- ✓ Ethical issues – conflicts of interest, fee levels.
- ✓ Compatible with audit firm's image or strategic plan.

5.6 Selection criteria (enterprise)

- ✓ Understanding of the business and management.
- ✓ Knowledge, understanding and experience of the business sectors operated in.
- ✓ Range and quality of services provided.
- ✓ Audit methodology used.
- ✓ Evidence of quality in work and services provided.
- ✓ Calibre and fit of proposed senior team members.
- ✓ Personal rapport – "chemistry".
- ✓ Standing of the audit firm.
- ✓ Ability to add value to the business.
- ✓ Competitive fees – fair, value for money.

6 LOWBALLING

- ✓ "Lowballing" or "predatory pricing" is where a firm seeks to increase its market share by dropping its quote for an audit fee to undercut its competitors
- ✓ Commercial reality.
- ✓ ACCA Code of Ethics does not specifically prohibit.
- ✓ Public perception that audit quality is reduced.
- ✓ Risk must be managed to ensure integrity and objectivity (independence) is not seen to be threatened.
- ✓ Audit quality must not be impaired by reduction in fees.

BUSINESS RISK

1 BUSINESS RISK

Results from significant conditions, events, circumstances, actions or inactions that could adversely affect the entity's ability to achieve its objectives and execute its strategies, or through the setting of inappropriate objectives and strategies.

Any event which may affect the entity's ability to survive and compete in its market as well as to maintain its financial strength, positive public image and the overall quality of its people and services".

1.1 Risk management

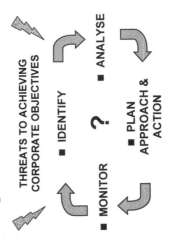

1.2 Types of risk

- ✓ Strategic (enterprise).
- ✓ Financial.
- ✓ Process (operational).
- ✓ Compliance.
- ✓ Environment.
- ✓ Information.
- ✓ Human capital.
- ✓ Integrity.
- ✓ Technological.
- ✓ Reputation.

1.3 Risk analysis

- ✓ Likelihood, impact.
- ✓ High, medium, low'

1.4 Risk management

- ✓ Transfer, Avoid, Reduce, Accept (TARA)

2 BUSINESS RISK AUDIT APPROACH

2.1 Nature

- ✓ Addresses how business risk could evolve into a risk of material misstatement in the financial statements (financial statement risk).

- ✓ Traditional audit concentrates on risks inherent in specific transactions – **bottom-up** approach.

BUSINESS RISK

✓ Business risk approach is a **top-down** approach driven by ISA 315 and ISA 330.

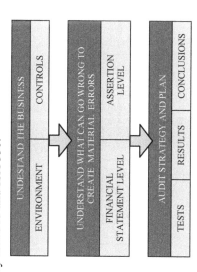

2.2 Rationale

✓ Effective – recognises impact of going concern, fraud, complexity of transactions, technology and globalisation.

✓ Efficient – changes in technology (used by both auditors and clients) and the nature of the information audited gives greater scope for audit effort to be devoted to higher level assessments.

✓ Improved client service – added value is recognised.

✓ Corporate governance input.

✓ Engagement risk can be lowered.

2.3 Top-down approach

✓ Takes into account the risks inherent to the entity and its environment, how such risks are managed and their potential impact on the financial statements.

✓ The auditor gains a greater understanding of management's current and future business strategy, core business processes, key performance indicators and associated risks and controls in place.

✓ Involves the auditor comparing the expectations developed that are based on this assessment with the performance and position reflected in the financial report.

✓ The approach identifies and focuses attention on key or "critical business" processes.

PLANNING, MATERIALITY AND RISK

1 PLANNING

1.1 Scope and objectives

✓ Planning entails developing:

- the overall audit strategy setting the scope, timing and direction of the audit; and
- a detailed approach for the nature, timing and extent of audit procedures in order to reduce audit risk to an acceptable low level – the audit plan.

Planning Objectives:
- To devote appropriate attention to important areas
- To identify potential problems and resolve on a timely basis
- To organise and manage the engagement in an effective and efficient way
- To assist in assigning, directing, supervising and reviewing audit

1.2 Professional scepticism

✓ Must be applied throughout the planning process.

✓ Ensures that:

- right level of professional judgement is used; and
- resources are allocated to high risk areas.

✓ Application of professional scepticism means:

- developing and applying a high degree of knowledge of the entity's business and operating environment;
- critically appraising and challenging management and their assertions;
- designing the nature, timing and extent of audit procedures that are responsive to assessed risks;
- designing audit procedures to find any evidence that would contradict management assertions; and
- revising the assessment of risks and modifying the audit approach as new or contradictory audit evidence becomes available.

PLANNING, MATERIALITY AND RISK

1.3 Activities

- Preliminary engagement activities (e.g. client relationship, compliance with ethical requirements, terms of engagement).
- Developing and documenting the overall audit strategy and detailed audit plan.
- Establishing the resources required.
- Direction, supervision and review of the audit team.
- Changing the strategy and plan as audit issues emerge.
- Communication to those charged with governance and management.

2 UNDERSTANDING THE ENTITY

The auditor should identify and assess risks of material misstatement, whether due to fraud or error, at the financial statement and assertion levels, through understanding the entity and its environment, including internal control, in order to design and implement responses to those risks.

2.1 Methods

- Inquire.
- Observe.
- Review, inspect, analyse.
- Analytical procedures, benchmarking.
- Audit team discussions about client and financial statements:
  - Susceptibility to material misstatements;
  - Susceptibility to fraud;
  - Application of the financial reporting framework;
  - Maintaining professional scepticism;
  - Staying alert for indications of fraud and error; and
  - Rigorous follow up and monitoring.

2.2 Using the understanding

- In addition to those uses already discussed:
  - Determine materiality levels;
  - Determine special audit considerations;
  - Analytical expectations;
  - Evaluate audit evidence;
  - Recognise conflicting information;
  - Making informed enquiries and discussions; and
  - Appraise accounting policies and disclosures.

3 ANALYTICAL PROCEDURES

3.1 At the planning stage

Meaning

- The analysis of significant ratios and trends including the resulting investigation of fluctuations and relationships:
  - that are inconsistent with other relevant information; or
  - which deviate from predictable amounts.

Purpose

- To assist in understanding the business.
- To identify areas of potential risk (e.g. financial condition).
- To plan nature, timing and extent of other audit procedures.

Based on

- Interim financial information.
- Budgets/forecasts and management accounts.
- Draft financial statements.
- Discussions with client.
- Understanding the entity and its environment.
- Ratio and trend analysis over several years

3.2 Expectations and performance measures

- Understanding the entity and planning analytical procedures establishes expectations about plausible relationships that are reasonably expected to exist.

- When such expectations are not met, consider potential increase in the risk of material misstatement.

- Professional scepticism must apply when, for example, the auditor is aware of the potential for pressure on management to meet expected performance measures.

PLANNING, MATERIALITY AND RISK

4 INTERNAL CONTROL

4.1 Elements

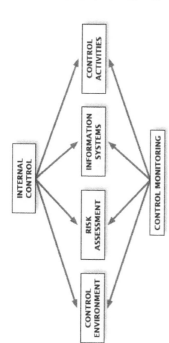

4.2 Understanding

- ✓ Design.
- ✓ Implementation.
- ✓ Poor design/implementation indicates increased risk of material misstatement.

4.3 Methods

- ✓ Previous experience of entity.
- ✓ Inquiry.
- ✓ Observation.
- ✓ Inspection.
- ✓ Walk-through.
- ✓ CAATs.
- ✓ Re-performance.
- ✓ Actions taken.
- ✓ Professional judgement.

5 INTERNAL AUDIT

5.1 Activities

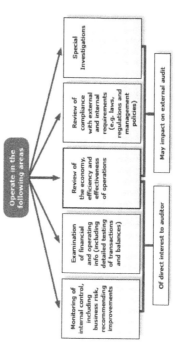

PLANNING, MATERIALITY AND RISK

5.2 Coordination of work

- ✓ Share information obtained for planning purposes.
- ✓ Discuss business developments.
- ✓ Discuss materiality, risk and audit objectives.
- ✓ Review work plans, programs and findings.
- ✓ Liaise on timing of internal audit work (so external auditor can use findings).

5.3 Basic principles

- ✓ Understand:
  - ➤ The role of internal audit;
  - ➤ Its insight into operations and business risks;
  - ➤ Work and results; and
  - ➤ Reports to those charged with governance.

- ✓ Determine:
  - ➤ Relevance of internal audit; and
  - ➤ Possible use of internal audit's work and its adequacy for the purpose of external audit.

5.4 Relying on the work of internal audit

- ✓ Obtain a sufficient understanding of internal audit activities:
  - ➤ to identify and assess the risk of material misstatement of the financial statements; and
  - ➤ to design and perform relevant audit procedures.

- ✓ Make a preliminary assessment of the internal audit function if relevant to the auditor's risk assessment:
  - ➤ Objectivity;
  - ➤ Competence; and a
  - ➤ Systematic and disciplined approach

- ✓ Determine effect on audit plan:
  - ➤ Nature/scope of internal audit work to be performed;
  - ➤ Assessed risks of material misstatement;
  - ➤ Degree of subjectivity and judgement involved in the evaluation of the audit evidence gathered by internal audit; and
  - ➤ The need to reperform work of internal audit.

PLANNING, MATERIALITY AND RISK

6 MATERIALITY

6.1 Levels of materiality

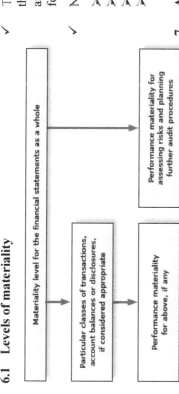

6.2 Planning materiality

✓ Quantitative factors:

- 5 – 10% profit;
- ½ – 1% net assets;
- 1 – 2% total assets; and
- ½ – 1 % revenue.

6.3 Performance materiality

✓ The amounts that reduce to an appropriately low level the probability (risk) that the aggregate of uncorrected and undetected misstatements could exceed materiality for the financial statements as a whole.

✓ Not simply a mechanical calculation, but draws upon:

- the nature of the entity;
- the auditor's past experience;
- the use of professional judgement; and
- the expectation of misstatements in the current period.

7 AUDIT RISK

7.1 Overview

✓ The risk that the auditor gives an inappropriate audit opinion when the financial statements are materially misstated.

7.2 Audit risk model

✓ Inherent risk + Control risk + Detection risk

✓ Detection risk has two components:

- Sampling risk; and
- Non-sampling risk.

7.3 Risk of material misstatement

- Risk that the financial statements will contain a material error prior to being audited.
- Derived from inherent risk and control risk.

7.4 Significant risks

- Those risks that relate to material non-routine transactions and judgemental matters where there is, for example;
  - greater ability for management intervention re accounting treatment;
  - greater ability to use manual override of internal controls;
  - complex calculations or accounting policies open to different interpretations;
  - subjective judgement based on a significant measurement uncertainty; and
  - the nature of the transactions makes it difficult to implement effective controls over the risks.
- Revenue is always considered to be a significant risk, unless clearly not.
- Any risk that relates to potential fraud is also considered to be a significant risk.

EVIDENCE

1 AUDIT EVIDENCE

- Sufficient appropriate audit evidence should be obtained, from which reasonable conclusions can be drawn, as a basis for the audit opinion.
- Audit evidence supports the auditor's opinion.
- Evidence is obtained from understanding the entity, tests of control and substantive procedures.

1.1 Sufficiency

- Sufficiency measures quantity of evidence required.

Factors

- Nature and level of inherent risk.
- Nature of internal control.
- Reliance on effective controls.
- Auditors' (cumulative) knowledge and experience.
- Materiality of items.
- Audit findings (e.g. fraud or error).
- Source and reliability of information (i.e. persuasiveness).

1.2 Appropriate

- Appropriateness measures quality (relates to relevance and reliability).

Relevance

- Supports financial statement assertions relating to:
  - recognition;
  - measurement; and
  - presentation/disclosure
- Three groups of assertions:
  (1) Transactions and events (completeness, occurrence, classification, cut-off, accuracy);
  (2) Account balances (existence, rights and obligations, completeness, valuation and allocation); and
  (3) Presentation and disclosure (occurrence, rights and obligations, completeness, classification, understandability, accuracy and valuation).

Reliability

- External more reliable than entity sources.
- Documentary/written more reliable than verbal/oral.
- Auditor obtained more reliable than indirectly obtained.
- Information more reliable when related internal controls are effective.
- Original documents more reliable than copies.
- Consistency increases persuasiveness.

EVIDENCE

1.3 Procedures

- Inspection (documents, records, physical assets, etc).
- Observation (of procedures and processes).
- Inquiry (of other parties both internal and external).
- Confirmation (from other parties of inquiries made).
- Recalculation (to confirm mathematical accuracy).
- Reperformance (to confirmed procedures performed).
- Analytical procedures (to establish relationships between data sets and develop expectations).

2 SUBSTANTIVE ANALYTICAL REVIEW

2.1 Approach

- Suitability (and sufficiency) of analytical procedures.
- Evaluate reliability of data.
- Develop expectations.
- Determine the amount of any difference that is acceptable without further investigation.

2.2 Suitability

- Good where an item can be verified directly by reference to another (valid, audited) item.
- Can provide corroborative evidence.
- May be particularly effective in testing for understatement.

2.3 Reliability of data

- Influenced by source and nature.
- Depends on the circumstances under which it is obtained.

Factors to consider

- Audit objectives and extent of reliance.
- Degree of disaggregation of available information.
- Availability of financial and non-financial data.
- Reliability of information available.
- Sources of information.
- Comparability of information.
- Knowledge previously gained.
- Nature of enterprise and its operations.
- Controls in operation.

2.4 Types of test

- Trend analysis.
- Ratio analysis.
- Reasonable test.

EVIDENCE

2.5 Extent of reliance

Factors to consider

- ✓ Materiality of items involved.
- ✓ Risk assessments.
- ✓ Accuracy with which expected results can be predicted.
- ✓ Degree to which information can be disaggregated.
- ✓ Availability of information.

Greatest use

- ✓ Existing, well established, client.
- ✓ Well-known, stable industry.
- ✓ Predictive information available.
- ✓ Effective accounting and internal control systems.

3 AUDIT SAMPLING

3.1 Basic principles

- ✓ Choose items appropriately to meet test objective:
  - ➢ all items (100%);
  - ➢ specific items (judgemental sampling); or
  - ➢ audit sampling (draw conclusion on population as a whole).

3.2 Terminology

Audit sampling

- ✓ Applying procedures to less than 100% of items.
- ✓ All sampling units have equal chance of selection.
- ✓ Forms a conclusion on population as a whole.

Error

- ✓ Control deviation (in tests of control).
- ✓ Misstatement (in a substantive procedure).

Anomalous error

- ✓ Arises from an isolated event.
- ✓ Not representative of errors in the population.

Population

- ✓ The entire set of data.

Sampling risk

- ✓ Possibility that auditor's conclusion, based on a sample, is inappropriate.

Confidence level

- ✓ The mathematical complement of risk (e.g. 5% risk ≡ 95% confidence).

EVIDENCE

Non-sampling risk

- ✓ The risk of an inappropriate conclusion for any reason not related to sample size.

Sampling unit

- ✓ Individual items in a population.

Statistical sampling

- ✓ Random selection of a sample.
- ✓ Use of probability theory to evaluate.

Stratification

- ✓ Dividing a population into sub-populations.

Tolerable misstatement

- ✓ Equates to performance materiality.

Tolerable rate of deviation

- ✓ The maximum acceptable failure rate of an internal control (usually zero).

3.3 Audit sampling

- ✓ Sample design.
- ✓ Sample selection.
- ✓ Audit procedures.
- ✓ Error evaluation.

3.4 Design

- ✓ Test objective.
- ✓ Nature of evidence required.
- ✓ Complete population.
- ✓ Characteristics of population.
- ✓ Deviation or misstatement characteristics.
- ✓ Combination of procedures required.

Sample size

- ✓ Reduce sampling risk to an acceptable level.
- ✓ Low sampling risk requires high sample size.
- ✓ Use of statistical means or professional judgement.

3.5 Sample selection

Random selection

- ✓ Random number tables or generator.
- ✓ Every item has an equal chance of being selected.

Systematic/interval sampling

- ✓ Constant selection interval.
- ✓ Unstructured population must be randomly distributed.
- ✓ Value-weighted selection.

EVIDENCE

Monetary unit sampling (MUS)

- ✓ Every $ unit has an equal chance of being selected.
- ✓ Higher value items have a greater chance of being selected (value-weighted).
- ✓ Every item value greater than the sampling interval will be selected.

Haphazard selection (not audit sampling)

- ✓ "Random" sampling but without use of tables or generator.
- ✓ Significant risk of intentional or unintentional bias.

Block sampling (not audit sampling)

- ✓ All items selected within a given range.
- ✓ Mainly used to test populations for completeness before sample selection.

Testing each item

- ✓ If an item is inappropriate, select another using same selection criteria.
- ✓ If test cannot be completed, alternative procedures should be implemented.
- ✓ If no alternative is available, treat test item as an error.

3.6 Results

- ✓ All errors and deviations must be analysed.
  - ➢ Nature and cause;
  - ➢ Potential effect on test objectives; and
  - ➢ Confirm or revise preliminary assessment of the population characteristics.

3.7 Error projection

- ✓ Monetary misstatements indicative of the population, extrapolate to the population.
- ✓ Isolated misstatements not indicative of the population should not be extrapolated.

3.8 Evaluation of results

Tests of control

- ✓ If control risk is higher than originally assessed:
  - ➢ extend sample size (statistical sampling approach);
  - ➢ test alternative controls; or
  - ➢ extend substantive procedures (judgemental approach).

Substantive procedures

- ✓ If substantive errors are considered to be material:
  - ➢ management should be requested to adjust; and
  - ➢ re-evaluate uncorrected misstatements.

EVIDENCE

3.9 Statistical sampling

✓ Involves:
  - random sample selection; and
  - probability theory for evaluation of results.

Attribute sampling

✓ Units have, or have not, an attribute (property).
✓ Driver is event occurrence, not monetary values.
✓ Used in tests of control.

Variables sampling

✓ Value within a continuous range.
✓ Conclusions based on monetary values.

3.10 Non-statistical sampling

✓ Everything else that is not statistical sampling

4 DOCUMENTATION

4.1 Importance

✓ Support audit opinion.
✓ Demonstrates compliance with ISAs.
✓ Assist in the planning and performance of the audit.
✓ Facilitate the supervision and review of audit work.
✓ Record the audit evidence.
✓ Must be sufficiently complete to provide an overall understanding of the audit.

4.2 Professional scepticism

✓ Thought and actions, reasoning and outcomes must all be documented.

4.3 Form and content

Matters to consider

✓ Nature of the engagement.
✓ Form of the auditor's report.
✓ Nature and complexity of organisation/control systems.
✓ Specific audit methodology.
✓ Standardisation.
✓ Extent of documentation prepared by the entity.
✓ Needs for direction, supervision and review of tasks assigned to assistants.

EVIDENCE

Techniques

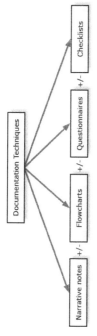

- Electronic files plus administration and control.

4.4 Confidentiality and safe custody

Confidentiality

- Confidentiality is a fundamental ethical principle.

Safe custody

- "24/7" restrictions and secure access.
- Standard data security principles apply for audit documentation in e-format.

4.5 Retention

- For a period:
  - sufficient to meet the needs of the audit practice; and
  - in accordance with legal and professional requirements.

ACCA recommended minimum

- Seven years for audit working papers.
- Seven years for tax files (then return to client).
- If stored electronically, standard security and backup procedures plus time lock to prevent early deletion.

4.6 Ownership

- Working papers are the auditor's property and are confidential.
- Inspection is at the auditor's discretion.

5 WRITTEN REPRESENTATIONS

5.1 Written representations

- A written statement by management to confirm certain matters or to support other audit evidence.
- Necessary information that the auditor requires.
- Often relate to areas of the audit that are:
  - subjective; and/or
  - dependent on management's responsibilities, judgement and actions (or lack of).
- Do not provide sufficient appropriate audit evidence on their own.

EVIDENCE

Audit objectives

- To obtain written representations that management (those charged with governance) has:
  - fulfilled its responsibility for preparing the financial statements; and
  - provided the auditor with complete information.
- To support other audit evidence relevant to assertions if necessary (or required by ISAs).
- To respond appropriately where written representations are not provided.

5.2 Procedure for obtaining

- Auditor prepares on client letterhead.
- Dated close to (before) the date of the audit report.
- Signed by those responsible for the financial statements:
  - CEO; and
  - Minuted by the board.

As audit evidence

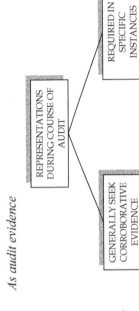

5.3 Essential management representations

- Responsibility for the preparation of the financial statements following the applicable framework.
- Provided all relevant information and access (e.g. to books, records and personnel).
- All transactions have been recorded and are reflected in the financial statements.

EVIDENCE

5.4 Other representations

- ✓ As required by ISAs.
- ✓ To support audit evidence already gathered.
- ✓ To confirm oral representations made by management:
  - ➤ Seek corroborative evidence;
  - ➤ Evaluate reasonableness/consistency; and
  - ➤ Consider whether individuals adequately informed.
- ✓ If necessary (material, other evidence cannot reasonably be expected to exist) obtain in writing. Confirming oral representations reduces risk of misunderstanding.

Specific instances

- ✓ May be the only audit evidence which can reasonably be expected to be available (e.g. management's intention to settle a legal claim out of court).
- ✓ In areas of understatement (e.g. liabilities, income, disclosures). Management represents that it is not aware of any understatement or non-disclosure.
- ✓ Where contradicted by other audit evidence:
  - ➤ Investigate as doubt must be resolved; and
  - ➤ Reliability of other representations may also be called into doubt.

5.5 Reliability of representations

- ✓ If in doubt reconsider original risk assessment.
- ✓ Where concerns about management's competence, integrity, ethics or diligence, consider reliability of:
  - ➤ representations; and
  - ➤ audit evidence in general.
- ✓ Auditor may:
  - ➤ issue a qualified opinion; or
  - ➤ issue a disclaimer; or
  - ➤ in extreme cases, withdraw from the engagement (if allowed to by law).
- ✓ Where significant doubt about representations on management's responsibilities, auditor should issue a disclaimer of opinion on the basis of unable to obtain sufficient appropriate audit evidence.

5.6 Refusal by management to provide representations

- ✓ Discuss the reasons why with management and those charged with governance.
- ✓ Establish if other audit evidence is available.
- ✓ If no satisfactory solution, consider implications for the audit report (e.g. disclaimer).

5.7 Typical other content

- ✓ Significant assumptions are reasonable.
- ✓ All events after the reporting date have been adjusted or disclosed (IAS 10).
- ✓ Effects of uncorrected misstatements are immaterial (individually and in aggregate).
- ✓ Appropriate selection and application of accounting policies.
- ✓ Appropriate classification of assets and liabilities.
- ✓ Plans or intentions that may affect the carrying amount or classification of assets and liabilities.
- ✓ Recognition, measurement and disclosure of all liabilities (actual and contingent).
- ✓ Title to assets pledged as security.
  - ➤ Aspects of laws, regulations and contractual agreements that may affect the financial statements, including non-compliance.

6 EXTERNAL CONFIRMATION

- ✓ The process of obtaining and evaluating a direct communication from a third party in response to a request for information affecting financial statement assertions.

6.1 Need for

- ✓ Factors to consider:
  - ➤ Materiality;
  - ➤ Risk of material misstatement;
  - ➤ Effectiveness of controls; and
  - ➤ Availability of other evidence to reduce audit risk.

6.2 Reliability

- ✓ External, direct, written.

6.3 Design of request

Confirming party

- ✓ Knowledge of subject matter.
- ✓ Ability and willingness to reply.

Positive

- ✓ Reply is expected.
- ✓ Preferred when risk is assessed as high.

Negative

- ✓ Only reply if disagreement.
- ✓ Consider when:
  - ➤ Strong internal controls;
  - ➤ Large number of small balances;
  - ➤ Errors not expected; and
  - ➤ Expectation that request will not be ignored.

EVIDENCE

Open

- Balance not shown.
- Respondent requested to provide information.
- Understatement approach (e.g. payables).

Closed

- Balance shown.
- Overstatement approach (e.g. receivables).

6.4 Confirmation process

- The auditor must control:
  - determination of information required;
  - selection process and who should confirm;
  - design of request;
  - sending requests; and
  - receiving responses.

- If management refuses to allow confirmation:
  - Assess reasonableness of refusal;
  - Re-assess risk of material misstatement;
  - Perform alternative procedures, if appropriate; and
  - Consider implications for audit report, if any.

6.5 Responses

Information given

- Expected individual and expected means.
- Consistency and reliability with other evidence.

Agreement

- Risk of tick box approach.

Disagreement

- Identify reason.
- Increased risk of material misstatement.
- Apply further audit procedures to obtain sufficient reliable audit evidence.

No response

- Consider use of alternative procedures.
- If insufficient, consider implications for audit report.

EVIDENCE

7 EXPERTS

7.1 Management's expert

Audit evidence

✓ Used by the entity to assist in preparing the financial statements.

▸ Asset/liability valuations;
▸ Assessment of quantities/condition of assets; and
▸ Legal services.

✓ Financial statement considerations:

▸ materiality;
▸ risk of material misstatement; and
▸ quality, quantity and cost of other evidence.

✓ Expert considerations:

▸ competence, capabilities and objectivity;
▸ understandability of the work carried out; and
▸ appropriateness of the work as audit evidence.

Competence

✓ Nature and level of experience of the expert.
✓ Qualifications, member of professional body, reputation.
✓ Previous experience or working with expert.

Capabilities

✓ Expert's ability to exercise his competence.
✓ Consider effect, if any, of management restrictions.

Objectivity

✓ Professional judgement free from bias, conflict of interest or influence of others.
✓ Consider threats to expert's objectivity (e.g. self-interest).

Field of expertise

✓ Relevance to audit assertions.
✓ Ability to evaluate expert's work and findings.
✓ Applicable professional standards or legal requirements.
✓ Assumptions and methods used.
✓ Nature of data used.
✓ Observation.
✓ Need to use auditor's expert to corroborate.

Source data

✓ Complete, sufficient, relevant, reliable, consistent.

EVIDENCE

Terms of reference

- Nature, scope and objectives of work.
- Assumptions and methods to be used.
- Access to records and employees.
- Respective roles and responsibilities.
- Nature, timing and extent of communications.
- Form/content of the expert's report (in writing) including limitations of use.

Assessing expert findings

- Relevance to financial statement assertions.
- Source data used.
- Assumptions used and consistency with prior years.
- Consistency with other sources of evidence.
- Auditor's overall knowledge and findings.
- Timing of work carried out.

7.2 Auditor's expert

Need

- To assist the auditor in obtaining sufficient appropriate audit evidence.
- Professional judgement used to determine if there is a need for an auditor's expert.

- Typically:
  - a specialist in the audit firm;
  - similar work as for management's expert; and
  - used to challenge the management's expert (if he cannot be relied on).

Competence, capabilities, objectivity

- Same as for any member of the audit team.
- If an external agent, still treat as if a member of the audit team.

Understanding the expertise of the expert

- Similar to management's expert.
- Prime difference is that the expert is a team member:
  - audit partner sets nature, timing, scope, extent and objectives (engagement letter if external agent); and
  - work will be supervised and reviewed.

Evaluation of expert's work

- Same approach as audit team.

EVIDENCE

7.3 Auditor's report

- No reference to expert in unmodified report, unless required by law.
- If report is modified, reference to the expert may be needed to clarify position. If so, permission of expert must be obtained.
  - If expert refuses, seek legal advice.
- If management unable/refuse to obtain expert evidence – unable to obtain sufficient appropriate audit evidence.
- If management refuse to accept auditor's expert opinions and adjust financial statements – material misstatement.

EVALUATION AND REVIEW

1 AUDIT COMPLETION

1.1 Need for

- Quality control process to ensure:
  - all work was carried out according to audit plan;
  - all material and contentious issues dealt with;
  - the audit report is consistent with work performed;
  - audit work supports the audit opinion; and
  - ethical matters have been considered for audit re-acceptance.

1.2 Content

- All critical matters, particularly matters requiring professional scepticism and judgement:
  - uncorrected misstatements;
  - going concern;
  - management estimations and assertions;
  - provisions and contingencies;
  - subsequent events;
  - compliance with reporting framework;
  - deficiencies (weakness) letter;
  - written representations; and
  - communications to those charged with governance.

- Key decisions on these areas are subject to challenge, negotiation and discussions with management. Should be adequately documented with:
  - conclusions reached; and
  - rationale for supporting such conclusions.

1.3 Tools

- Professional scepticism.
- Review procedures.
- Completion checklists (supervisor, manager, partner, second partner review).
- Final analytical procedures.
- Disclosure checklists (e.g. IFRS, stock exchange, corporate governance).
- Points for Partner (other names include: Matters for Attention of Partner, Final Review Notes, Contentious Issues).
- Audit team challenged about adequacy and professionalism of their work.

EVALUATION AND REVIEW

1.4 Reviews

- Audit section review by senior/supervisor.
- Audit file and senior's work reviewed by manager.
- Engagement partner.
- Second partner review (pre-issuance, hot, high-risk).
- Technical review.
- Quality control review (post-issuance, cold).
- Regulator review (FRC, ACCA).

2 OPENING BALANCES

2.1 Audit objectives

- Do not contain errors that materially affect current financial statements.
- Appropriate accounting policies are consistently applied (or changes properly accounted for and adequately disclosed).

2.2 Procedures

Prior reporting period audited by another auditor

- Opening balances are not "re-audited".
- Review most recent financial statements and auditor's report for information relevant to opening balances, including disclosures.
- Review predecessor auditor's working papers, if available.

Prior period's auditor's report modified

- Impact (if any) of matters which resulted in a prior year modified report.

Current assets and liabilities

- The collection (payment) of opening accounts receivable (payable) provides evidence of the existence, rights and obligations, completeness, cut-off and valuation of the opening balances.
- Sales at the beginning of the period relate to net realisable value of inventory.
- Opening inventory.
  - Observe a current physical inventory count;
  - Reconcile back to opening quantities; and
  - Test valuation of opening items, gross profit and cut-off.
- Opening non-current assets and liabilities.
  - Reconcile closing balances and movements in year to opening balances;
  - examine underlying records (e.g. fixed asset registers);
  - third party confirmation (e.g. for long-term debt and investments).

EVALUATION AND REVIEW

2.3 Audit report

✓ Insufficient appropriate audit evidence:

➢ qualified opinion ("except for"): or
➢ disclaimer of opinion (material and pervasive).

✓ Opening balances containing misstatements which could materially affect the current period's financial statements will result in a:

➢ qualified opinion ("except for"): or
➢ adverse opinion (material and pervasive).

3 COMPARATIVES

3.1 Reporting frameworks

✓ Corresponding figures.
✓ Comparative financial statements.

3.2 Auditor responsibilities

✓ Agreeing correct reporting and appropriate classification, for example:

➢ accounting policies are consistent;
➢ figures agree; and
➢ appropriate disclosures made.

3.3 Reporting

Corresponding figures

✓ Prior period modification resolved:

  ▲ Usually no reference in report.
  ▲ But may be included in an emphasis of matter.

✓ Prior period modification unresolved:

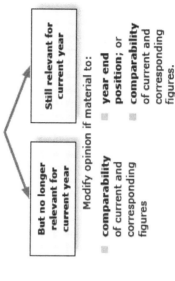

EVALUATION AND REVIEW

4 OTHER INFORMATION

4.1 Procedures

✓ Obtain and read the other information to identify any material inconsistencies or misstatement of facts.

Inconsistency

✓ Information contained in the financial statements is contradicted by the other information.

✓ If in financial statements and management refuses to change – modify audit opinion.

✓ If in other information and management refuses to change:

➢ discuss with those charged with governance;
➢ other matters paragraph; or
➢ withhold auditor's report; and
➢ consider withdrawal from engagement after obtaining legal advice.

Misstatement of fact

✓ Discuss with management.
✓ Ask management to consult with an external expert.
✓ Raise issue with those charged with governance.
✓ If no change made, seek legal advice.

5 SUBSEQUENT EVENTS

5.1 Events after the reporting period

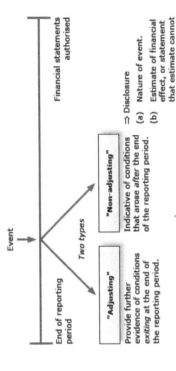

⇒ Disclosure
(a) Nature of event.
(b) Estimate of financial effect, or statement that estimate cannot be made.

5.2 Audit procedures and effect on report

✓ Understand management's systems for identifying adjusting and non-adjusting subsequent events.

EVALUATION AND REVIEW

Before date of audit report – active responsibility

- ˅ Enquire of management, those charged with governance and other relevant third parties.
- ˅ Review board minutes/correspondence.
- ˅ Review of after-date cash books, transactions, journals and other records for material/unusual items.
- ˅ Review of budgets, cash flow forecasts and management reports.
- ˅ Inquire of lawyers concerning litigation and claims.
- ˅ If no change made for material items, qualified or adverse audit opinion.

After date of audit report – before financial statements issued

- ˅ No active audit role – would only consider if aware (e.g. informed by management as required by letter of engagement).
- ˅ Auditors should discuss with management and take action appropriate in the circumstances.

If financial statements

Amended
- ➤ Withdraw old audit report.
- ➤ Extend audit procedures, including subsequent events review, to new date.
- ➤ Issue new report when financial statements approved.

Not amended
(auditor thinks they should be)
- ➤ Discuss with those charged with governance.
- ➤ If no adjustment, withdraw old audit report.
- ➤ Issue new report expressing a qualified or adverse opinion.

- ˅ If amended financial statements issued, without new report, seek legal advice how to prevent reliance on report.

After financial statements issued

- ˅ If auditor becomes aware of a fact which existed at the date of the report which, if known at that date, may have caused a modified report:
  - ➤ Take legal advice on what action may be taken;
  - ➤ Discuss with management; and
  - ➤ Take appropriate action as allowed by law.

EVALUATION AND REVIEW

6 GOING CONCERN

6.1 IAS 1 presentation of financial statements

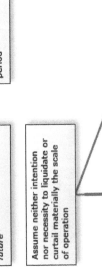

6.2 Responsibilities

Management

✓ To assess ability to continue as a going concern.

Auditor's responsibilities

✓ Consider appropriateness of use of going concern assumption when planning, conducting and evaluating the results of audit procedures.

✓ Consider whether material uncertainties relating to the going concern assumption require disclosure.

6.3 Planning considerations

✓ Understand and assess the process used by management to assess going concern.

✓ If no formal process, discuss with management and make appropriate enquiries.

✓ Identify events/conditions that may cast significant doubt on ability to continue as a going concern.

Financial indicators of significant doubt

✓ Net liability/net current liability position.
✓ Withdrawal of financial support.
✓ Negative operating cash flows.
✓ Adverse key financial ratios.
✓ Substantial operating losses.
✓ Significant deterioration in value of assets.
✓ Arrears or discontinuance of dividends.
✓ Inability to pay creditors on due dates.
✓ Difficulty in complying with terms of loan agreements.
✓ Change from credit to cash-on-delivery terms.

EVALUATION AND REVIEW

Operational indicators

- Intention to cease operations.
- Loss of key management without replacement.
- Loss of a major market, license, principal supplier, key customer (no appropriate alternatives).
- Labour difficulties or shortages of key supplies.
- Fundamental change to which the entity cannot adequately respond.

Other indicators

- Non-compliance with capital, statutory, regulatory requirements.
- Pending legal proceedings that may bankrupt the entity.
- Changes in legislation or government policy.
- Uninsured/underinsured catastrophes.

Mitigating factors

- Management's plans:
  - Disposal of assets;
  - Debt rescheduling;
  - Obtaining capital; and
  - Continued support.

Throughout the audit.

- Keep alert for events and conditions that affect going concern. If identified:
  - perform additional procedures; and
  - reassess audit risk.

6.4 Audit evidence

Sources of information

- Client's system for timely identification of warnings of risks/uncertainties.
- Budgets, forecast information.
- Obligations, undertakings, guarantees with lenders, suppliers.
- Bank borrowing facilities and suppliers' credit.
- Management's plans for future action.

Specific procedures

- Analyse management's assessment:
  - assessment process;
  - assumptions used;
  - plan for future action; and
  - feasible in the circumstances.

EVALUATION AND REVIEW

- Analyse cash flow, profit and other relevant forecasts.
- Analyse latest available interim statements.
- Breaches of debentures and loan agreements.
- Financing difficulties noted in minutes of meetings.
- Existence of litigation and claims and the reasonableness of management's assessments.
- Third party continued support.
- Order books.
- Subsequent events review.
- Existence, terms and adequacy of borrowing facilities.
- Obtaining and reviewing reports of regulatory actions.
- Adequacy of any planned disposals of assets.
- General written representation – use of going concern assumption.
- Specific written representations – plans that might have a significant effect on solvency in foreseeable future.

6.5 Cash flows

Considerations

- Control systems that generate cash flow detail.
- Appropriateness of underlying assumptions.
- Additional facts/information since forecast prepared.
- Comparison to historic budgets, forecasts, etc
- Comparison to current period with results achieved to date.

6.6 Beyond the assessment period

- Inquire of management (and obtain a written representation) if indicators of significant doubt beyond the period of assessment.

6.7 Conclusions and Reporting

Basic principle

- The auditor should judge whether material uncertainty about the going concern assumption exists.

Going concern is appropriate and no uncertainty

- Statement that the financial statements have been prepared on the going concern basis.
- No reference made in the auditor's report.

EVALUATION AND REVIEW

Going concern is appropriate, but a material uncertainty exists

✓ Adequate description and disclosure of:
  ➢ events or conditions giving rise to the doubt; and
  ➢ management's plans to alleviate the uncertainty.

✓ Statement that:
  ➢ there is material uncertainty;
  ➢ entity may be unable to realise assets; and
  ➢ discharge liabilities in normal course of business.

✓ If **adequate** disclosure:
  ➢ express an **unmodified** opinion; plus
  ➢ Emphasis of Matter paragraph.

Emphasis of Matter

Without qualifying our opinion we draw attention to Note X to the financial statements. [Summary of matter]

✓ If clearly **inadequate** or **no** disclosure made express an **adverse** opinion.

Basis for Adverse Opinion

[Description of events that indicate material uncertainty.] The financial statements do not disclose this fact.

Adverse Opinion

In our opinion, **because of the omission** of the information mentioned in the Basis for Adverse Opinion paragraph, the financial statements do **not** give a true and fair view …

✓ If insufficient detail disclosed, express a qualified opinion.

Basis for Qualified Opinion

[Description] The financial statements fail to fully disclose this fact.

Qualified Opinion

In our opinion, **except for the incomplete disclosure** ….

Going concern assumption is inappropriate

✓ Adverse audit opinion.

Management is unwilling or unable to assess

✓ Qualified or disclaimer of opinion as insufficient appropriate audit evidence obtained.

Communication with those charged with governance

✓ Report any events which may cast doubt on ability to continue as a going concern.

AUDIT OF FINANCIAL STATEMENTS

1 AUDIT AREAS

1.1 Considerations

Is the matter expected to be material?

- ✓ Quantitatively or qualitatively? Do not forget disclosures.
- ✓ Has it been material historically? Is there any reason for it to have changed this year?
- ✓ Calculate **relevant** materiality as part of your answer.

What are the relevant accounting standards?

- ✓ IFRS, IFRIC or best practice if not yet subject to any particular IFRS.
- ✓ Local legislative requirements or other Regulatory requirements (e.g. Stock Exchange rules).

Which financial statement assertions that are most at risk?

- ✓ Completeness, occurrence, accuracy, cut-off, classification, presentation & disclosure, appropriate carrying amount, rights and obligations, existence.

What evidence is expected to be available?

- ✓ Internal or external?
- ✓ Written or oral?
- ✓ Direct or indirect?

Impact on audit report

- ✓ Modified opinion.
- ✓ Emphasis of matter/Other matter paragraph.

2 ASSETS

2.1 Plant, property and equipment

Materiality

- ✓ In most enterprises, will be material.

Relevant accounting standards

- ✓ IAS 16 *Property, Plant and Equipment*
- ✓ IAS 17 *Leases*
- ✓ IAS 20 *Accounting for Government Grants and Disclosures of Government Assistance*
- ✓ IAS 23 *Borrowing Cost*
- ✓ IAS 36 *Impairment of Assets*
- ✓ IAS 37 *Provisions, Contingent Liabilities and Contingent Assets*
- ✓ IFRS 5 *Non-current Assets Held for Sale and Discontinued Operations*

AUDIT OF FINANCIAL STATEMENTS

Assertions most at risk

- Completeness – capital expenditure capitalised and not written off.
- Occurrence – of additions, disposals and impairment.
- Valuation – measurement of initial expenditure.
- Valuation (subsequent):
  - Appropriateness and accuracy of depreciation;
  - Impairment if necessary;
  - Revaluation of entire class of asset;
  - Revaluation/impairment accounting; and
  - Assets held for sale (IFRS 5).
- Presentation – movements in property, plant and equipment and correct classification. Additional disclosures if revaluation method used.
- Rights/obligations – consider lease agreements to ensure if nature of a finance lease, then an asset.
- Existence – physically inspected by the auditor.

Evidence

- Fixed asset register.
- Invoices for additions, disposals, repairs/improvements, other commissioning costs, own constructed assets (timesheets and costing records).
- Professionally carried out valuations.
- Budgets, forecasts, strategic plans, planned asset management decisions, to support useful life.
- Plant/production management with whom valuation and use issues can be discussed.
- Held for sale assets are available for immediate sale in present condition and that sale is highly probable:
  - management intentions, plans, board minutes;
  - management actions;
  - asking price is reasonable;
  - expected to be sold within one year; and
  - proof of after-date disposal.
- Estimate of fair value.

2.2 Intangible assets

Materiality

- Most likely in group accounts following acquisition of company with previously unrecognised intangible.
- Deferred development expenditure is a highly material asset in the pharmaceuticals sector.

1102

©2015 DeVry/Becker Educational Development Corp. All rights reserved.

AUDIT OF FINANCIAL STATEMENTS

Relevant accounting standards

- ✓ IAS 38 *Intangible Assets*
- ✓ IAS 36 *Impairment of Assets*

Assertions most at risk

- ✓ Occurrence – as for non-current assets especially impairment of development expenditure assets as a result of technical or market changes.
- ✓ Valuation (initial measurement) – must meet all of the strict conditions for asset recognition. Where valuation models used, test the reasonableness of the assumptions used and the correct application of the model.
- ✓ Presentation – with the required disclosures of IAS 38.
- ✓ Valuation (subsequent) – useful life:
  - ➤ finite may be difficult to estimate (include in written representation);
  - ➤ indefinite requires annual impairment review.
- ✓ Rights – difficult as no physical form.
- ✓ Existence:
  - ➤ Documents of title and similar.
  - ➤ Physical inspection of results of development work.
  - ➤ Carrying amount must be recoverable through future economic benefits, otherwise impairment.

Evidence

- ✓ Specialist valuations.
- ✓ Management representations, corporate plans, etc that confirm the period of economic life.
- ✓ Market research studies, correspondence with potential customers, initial orders placed.
- ✓ Invoices and time sheets for the costs that have been incurred and capitalised.

2.3 Goodwill

Materiality

- ✓ Can be high where based on "human capital" rather than other tangible assets.
- ✓ Can be highly subjective and often difficult to identify with reasonable precision, resulting in a high risk of material error.

Relevant accounting standards

- ✓ IFRS 3 *Business Combinations*
- ✓ IAS 36 *Impairment of Assets*

Assertions most at risk

- ✓ Completeness – of amortisation, or perhaps impairment, may be of concern.

AUDIT OF FINANCIAL STATEMENTS

- Valuation (initial measurement):
  - Provisions set up for "restructuring".
  - Inappropriate application of the detailed fair value rules of IFRS 3.
  - Inappropriate use of present values and expected values to the calculation of the fair value of deferred (and possibly contingent, consideration).
  - Recognition and measurement of intangible assets not recognised in the individual financial statements of the newly-acquired component (e.g. customer lists, contingent liabilities).
  - Appropriate allocation of goodwill to a cash generating unit (not necessarily related to the component acquired) – CGU.
- Valuation (subsequent) for example:
  - Correct application of impairment tests where evidence exists of impairment;
  - Correct approach to impairment when non-controlling interests are valued at the proportionate share of the identifiable net assets; and
  - Appropriateness of management's assertion of indefinite useful life.
- Rights/obligations – obligation to restructure an acquired business will have to be tested in line with the requirements of IFRS 3 (and IAS 37).
- Existence:
  - What type of investment is being accounted for – subsidiary, associate, joint venture (JV), special purpose entity (SPE).
  - Share certificates, and confirmation of entries in the investee's share register.

Evidence

- Legal correspondence and fee notes.
- Specialists and "due diligence" reports to assess fair values of assets and liabilities and useful economic life of resulting goodwill.
- Firm plans and costing for any restructuring provisions.

New acquisition – evidence

- Board minutes and agreements between the parties identify the date that control was obtained.
- Legal correspondence to confirm the substance of the acquisition.
- Purchase consideration (at fair value):

AUDIT OF FINANCIAL STATEMENTS

- ➤ Cash records, share price, contract detailing deferred and contingent consideration.
- ➤ Fair value calculation of deferred consideration, basis of discount rate and ability to pay, if cash.
- ➤ Terms of contingent consideration (earn-out).

✓ Assets and liabilities acquired (at fair value):

- ➤ A statement of financial position at the date of acquisition, or calculations supporting pro-rated result for the year, to attribute net asset values at date of acquisition.
- ➤ Ensure identified assets and liabilities have been valued according to IFRS 3 fair value guidance.
- ➤ If reliance placed on specialist reports for asset and liability valuations, apply ISA 500 and ISA 620.
- ➤ Other "due diligence" reports to help assess fair values of assets and liabilities and potential for impairment at some stage in the future.
- ➤ Assess management's procedures to identify all assets and liabilities (including contingent liabilities).

✓ Component's plans, costings and management approval (before commencement of the acquisition process) for restructuring provisions.

✓ That all acquisition costs have been charged directly through the acquirer's profit or loss and are not capitalised as part of goodwill.

On-going goodwill – evidence

✓ Understanding entity and its environment to identify indicators of goodwill impairment.

✓ Management's annual review for impairment of goodwill and reperformance:

- ➤ Testing CGUs with goodwill;
- ➤ Timing of impairment tests;
- ➤ Impaired goodwill allocated to non-controlling interests;
- ➤ Disposal of operation within a CGU to which goodwill has been allocated.

✓ Recalculation and correct treatment (through profit or loss) of the unwinding of the discount rate on fair value for deferred consideration.

2.4 Investment properties

Materiality

- ✓ Will be for property company (income also).

Relevant accounting standards

- ✓ IAS 40 *Investment Property*;
- ✓ IAS 16 *Property, Plant and Equipment*.
- ✓ IAS 36 *Impairment of Assets* for "cost model".

Assertions most at risk

- ✓ Completeness (e.g. rental income and gains/losses from fair value re-measurement).
- ✓ Occurrence – fall in fair values (or impairment) if the cost model is used. Client may be reluctant to admit.
- ✓ Valuation – follow IAS 16 re initial measurement. Subsequent expenditure – does it enhance or simply restore the originally assessed economic benefits?
- ✓ Presentation – transfers in or out of investment properties.
- ✓ Valuation (subsequent).
- ✓ Rights – IAS 17 may on occasion cause some difficulty.

Evidence

- ✓ Real estate agent's contracts and completion statements.
- ✓ Legal documents confirming transfer of title, risks and rewards.
- ✓ Real estate agent's/property valuer's reports.
- ✓ Board minutes.
- ✓ The receipt of rental income can be verified by reference to rental contracts and bank account entries.
- ✓ Analytical procedures for rental income.

2.5 Investments

Materiality

- ✓ Unless investment company, unlikely to be material.

Relevant accounting standards

- ✓ IAS 40 *Investment Property* – for real estate
- ✓ IAS 36 *Impairment of Assets*
- ✓ IAS 27 *Separate Financial Statements* – requires an investment in a subsidiary, associate or joint venture to be accounted for at cost or in accordance with IFRS 9.
- ✓ IFRS 9 *Financial Instruments*

AUDIT OF FINANCIAL STATEMENTS

Assertions most at risk

- Completeness – of dividend income and related enhancements (rights, bonuses, etc).
- Valuation (initial measurement) – acquisition (transaction) expenses should be included as part of the cost of acquisition when first recognised.
- Valuation (subsequent) – disclosure (or accounting for under IFRS 9) of fair values of investments at the year end or use of fair value models for unlisted investments.
- Presentation – IAS 32 and IFRS 7 checklists.

Evidence

- Broker's purchase/sale contract notes supported by authority to purchase/dispose (e.g. in board minutes).
- Securities certificates – may be held by bank or solicitor.
- Stock Exchange quotations at the reporting date.
- Independent information services (e.g. Moody's) to agree the events during the year (dividends declared, payment date, rights or scrip issues, stock splits, etc).
- Income received (verified by reference to published reference guides) corroborates existence and ownership.
- Management representation (e.g. about intention to hold or sell).

2.6 Inventories

Materiality

- For trading/manufacturing companies, high.

Relevant accounting standards

- IAS 2 *Inventories*.
- IAS 23 *Borrowing Costs*.

Assertions most at risk

- Completeness – double counting during physical count.
- Cut-off – deliberate procedures to manipulate profits.
- Omission – when items are in transit between locations or held at third party premises.
- Valuation (initial measurement) – application of appropriate cost formulas to obtain an approximation to cost.
- Valuation (subsequent) – lower of cost and net realisable value (NRV).
- Rights – "Reservation of Title" clauses.
- Existence – inventories held at third parties.

AUDIO OF FINANCIAL STATEMENTS

Evidence

- ✓ Inventory count observation instructions from client.
- ✓ Attendance at physical count.
- ✓ Third-party confirmations.
- ✓ Use of experts.
- ✓ Count sheets, inventory records, costing records, raw material purchase invoices, overhead expenses and apportionment, payroll and timesheets.
- ✓ After date sales invoices and pricing lists.
- ✓ Cut off – GRNs, despatch and WIP records.
- ✓ Subsequent events indicating NRV difficulties.
- ✓ Returns, warranty claims.
- ✓ Analytical procedures.
- ✓ Perpetual inventory counting system.

2.7 Receivables

Materiality

- ✓ If granting of credit is normal business practice, it is likely that the total of trade receivables will be material.

Relevant accounting standards

- ✓ IAS 1 *Presentation of Financial Statements* current and non-current distinctions.
- ✓ IAS 21 *The Effects of Changes in Foreign Exchange Rates* retranslation at year end using closing rate.

Assertions most at risk

- ✓ Completeness – recording of the related revenue and any related allowance for doubtful debts.
- ✓ Occurrence – as occurrence is confirmed when cash is received, only those sales made and not yet paid require confirmation of occurrence.
- ✓ Cut-off – link to inventory and sales.
- ✓ Presentation – the identification and separate disclosure of any receivables due after more than 12 months may be an issue.
- ✓ Valuation (subsequent) – bad debts.
- ✓ Rights – unless the company has factored any of its receivables, there is not usually any issue as to the rights to receive the benefit from the debt.
- ✓ Existence – the potential for overstated trade receivables (that do not exist) may arise.

Evidence

- Aged debtors listing.
- Direct confirmation letters.
- Dispute correspondence.
- Invoices, contracts, orders, despatch notes, correspondence, credit reports, remittance advices.

2.8 Cash and bank balances

Materiality

- Cash-in-hand and bank balances are not usually material, but susceptible to theft.
- Regard as material "by nature".

Relevant accounting standards

- There is no IFRS dealing uniquely with cash and bank.

Assertions most at risk

- Completeness – bank overdraft.
- Occurrence – opening/closing accounts, charging or crediting interest and exceptional banking activities.
- Valuation – conversion of foreign balances.
- Presentation – no offset unless agreed by bank.
- Rights/obligations – possible use of a company bank account for laundering money.

Evidence

- All bank statements on all accounts open/closed.
- Standard bank enquiry letter.
- Bank reconciliations.
- Cash book(s) and systems.
- Petty cash vouchers/operation of an imprest system.
- Physical counting of cash.
- Board minutes (authorising cheque signatories).
- Direct debit (DD)/standing order (SO) mandates.
- "Proof in total" – interest payable/receivable.

Bank reports for audit purposes

- Balances on accounts.
- Facilities – loans/overdrafts/guarantees.
- Securities (including set-off arrangements).
- Additional banking relationships.

Supplementary information may include:

- Trade finance – letters of credit, acceptances, bills, bonds, guarantees and indemnities.
- Derivatives and commodity trading – foreign exchange contracts, forward rate agreements, etc.
- Custodian arrangements – assets held but not charged.
- Other information (e.g. authorised signatories).

AUDIT OF FINANCIAL STATEMENTS

Bank disclaimers

- ✓ Standard wording on most replies from bank.

3 LIABILITIES

3.1 Lease obligations

Materiality

- ✓ Often monetarily material.
- ✓ Disclosures of obligations for non-cancellable operating leases provide a user with a highly material indication of the true level of a company's gearing.

Relevant accounting standards

- ✓ IAS 17 *Leases*.
- ✓ IAS 16 *Property, Plant and Equipment*.

Assertions most at risk

- ✓ Completeness – finance leases may be argued to be operating, thus off statement of financial position.
- ✓ Classification/valuation – whether to recognise a new lease arrangement as operating or finance.
- ✓ Presentation – disclosures are extensive. Checklist essential.
- ✓ Valuation (subsequent) – interest rate implicit in the lease.
- ✓ Rights/obligations – look to the substance of the agreement plus risks and rewards.
- ✓ Existence – external confirmation with the leasing company to confirm details of the agreement.

Evidence

- ✓ Terms of lease contract.
- ✓ Correspondence with leasing company and legal advisers.
- ✓ Revenue expenditure (e.g. insurance, maintenance, repairs).

3.2 Taxation (including deferred taxation)

Materiality

- ✓ Current taxation balance may not be material. Deferred tax may be.
- ✓ The tax expense (current plus deferred plus adjustments) would usually be material.

Relevant accounting standards

- ✓ IAS 12 *Income Taxes*

AUDIT OF FINANCIAL STATEMENTS

Assertions most at risk

- Completeness – risk of understatement of the liability if all differences between the carrying amount and the tax base of assets and liabilities are not identified.
- Valuation – recognition of a deferred tax asset; what tax rate to use to apply to the temporary differences.
- Presentation – as required by IAS 12.
- Allocation and valuation (subsequent) – impairment of deferred tax asset.

Evidence

- Tax computations and review by audit firm's own specialists.
- Correspondence with tax authorities.
- Deferred taxation working schedule.

3.3 Provisions

Materiality

- Dependent on industry and circumstances.
- Application of IFRS 1.
- Calculation may be subjective.

Relevant accounting standards

- IAS 37 *Provisions, Contingent Liabilities and Contingent Assets*

Assertions most at risk

- Completeness – understatement may be difficult to audit. Legal obligations are usually evidenced, constructive obligations not so.
- Occurrence – difficulty in establishing the trigger event for a provision.
- Valuation (initial measurement) – whether or not a provision should be recognised and if so, how much.
  - Discounting where the effect is material.
  - Expected value methods, where the provision concerns future events of some uncertainty.
- Presentation – movements in each provision are required to be disclosed.
- Allocation and valuation (subsequent) – calculation and disclosure of the "unwinding" of the discount rate.
- Obligations – fundamental.
- Existence – "big bath" provisions, risk of profit smoothing.

AUDIT OF FINANCIAL STATEMENTS

Evidence

- ✓ Correspondence files – legal, insurers, specialists.
- ✓ Schedule for each provision – b/f, increases during year, utilised during year, interest, reversals and c/f.
- ✓ Need to re-perform provision from first principles.

3.4 Pension funds

Materiality

- ✓ Defined contribution schemes – likely to be immaterial.
- ✓ Defined benefit schemes – funding liabilities on whole firm schemes are likely to be material.

Relevant accounting standards

- ✓ IAS 19 *Employee Benefits* and IAS 37 *Provisions, Contingent Liabilities and Contingent Assets*

Assertions most at risk

- ✓ Completeness – funding requirements may be underestimated, elements may be omitted and calculations are complicated.
- ✓ Valuation – complex procedures for calculation of liabilities. Need to rely on an expert.
- ✓ Presentation – extensive requirements.

Evidence

- ✓ Review board minutes, company secretarial minutes, employee contracts of employment, salary records and bank payments to identify new post-employment benefits and changes made to established benefits.
- ✓ Wages and salaries audit confirming calculations and deductions of pension benefits and payment to schemes (to include analytical review).
- ✓ Actuary's report – reliance on the use of an expert. Includes assumptions, agreement to company records, verifying market values, agreement of fair values.
- ✓ Application in accordance with IAS 19, treatment of net gains and losses, calculation and treatment.

3.5 Payables

Materiality

- ✓ In total, may be material. Individually, not so.

Relevant accounting standards

- ✓ No specific IFRS – IAS 1, IAS 21 and IAS 28 all deal with payables as they do with receivables. IAS 32 and IFRS 9 deal with presentation and measurement of debt and convertible debt.

AUDIT OF FINANCIAL STATEMENTS

Assertions most at risk

- Completeness – as with all liabilities, can be high risk.
- Cut-off – failure to accrue for goods received just before the year end, but not invoiced until after the year end.
- Presentation – ensuring correct analysis between < 12 months and > 12 months.
- Valuation – closing rate foreign currency retranslation.
- Existence – fraud risk of fictitious suppliers and related transactions.

Evidence

- Suppliers' statements, invoices, credit notes and clients' GRNs and purchase requisitions.
- Supplier confirmations and other correspondence.
- Bank records confirming payments made, especially after the year end.
- Detailed cut-off testing.
- Intermediaries (e.g. warehousing agents).
- Analytical procedures.

4 EVENTS

4.1 Revenue from contracts with customers

Materiality

- For trading entities, total revenue will be material.
- Transactions with a particular customer over the year may be material.
- ISA 240 considers revenue to be a significant risk.

Relevant accounting standards

- IFRS 15 *Revenue from Contracts with Customers*

Assertions most at risk

- Completeness – usually tested for understatement (related trade receivables for overstatement) but also overstatement if specific risk identified.
- Cut-off – must tie in with inventory, receivables.
- Occurrence – client deliberately overstates revenue.
- Valuation (initial measurement) – cut-off, deferred payment terms, barter transactions, use of fair value to measure revenue.
- Presentation – extensive IFRS 15 requirements.

AUDIT OF FINANCIAL STATEMENTS

Evidence

- Confirmation.
- Contracts, orders, invoices, signed despatch notes, reciprocal populations (e.g. purchases of for sale items).
- Substantive analytical review.
- Correspondence.

4.2 Segment reporting

Materiality

- By definition and IFRS requirements, segments are material.

Relevant accounting standards

- IFRS 8 *Operating Segments*

Assertions most at risk

- Valuation and allocation (measurement, recognition):
  - Based on management information reported to the chief operating decision maker (CODM).
  - Management information may not be supported by robust processes/controls or externally audited.
  - Underperforming segments must be shown separately.
  - Completeness – commercially sensitive or potentially detrimental segment information may be omitted.
  - Accuracy – information presented to management must meet the accepted criteria for useful information.
  - Understandability – clear and informative.
  - Presentation – extensive requirements of IFRS 8.

Evidence

- Identification of CODM.
- Understanding of internal management reporting system.
- Results of testing the reporting system's controls.
- Established segments and new segments realised in the year with supporting criteria.
- Agreement of quantitative disclosures to the CODM reporting detail with overall reconciliation to relevant totals in the financial statements (e.g. sales, profit or loss, assets).
- Consideration of qualitative disclosures supported by audit evidence already on file.
- Comparison to prior year to ensure consistency (or improvement) of disclosure.
- Disclosure checklist and management representations.

AUDIT OF FINANCIAL STATEMENTS

4.3 Borrowing costs

Materiality

- ✓ The amount capitalised on qualifying assets is unlikely to be material to the statement of financial position.
- ✓ The effect of capitalisation on "Interest expense" may be highly material to profit or loss and some ratios (e.g. interest cover).
- ✓ Capitalised can affect compliance with ratios relevant to a loan covenant.

Relevant accounting standards

- ✓ IAS 23 *Borrowing Costs*

Assertions most at risk

- ✓ Completeness – over capitalisation of interest on qualifying assets is more likely the risk.
- ✓ Occurrence – interest costs on external financing were incurred. Construction work has commenced (and not been suspended or completed).
- ✓ Valuation (initial costs) – appropriate interest rate and the qualifying expenditure.
- ✓ Presentation – disclosures of IAS 23.

Evidence

- ✓ Bank statements and other interest payments.
- ✓ Bank and other loan agreements to confirm interest rates.
- ✓ Construction costing records, fixed asset cost records or inventory records, to confirm borrowing requirement.

4.4 Government grants

Materiality

- ✓ Cash receipts can be highly material to a relatively new enterprise.

Relevant accounting standards

- ✓ IAS 20 *Accounting for Government Grants and Disclosure of Government Assistance*

Assertions most at risk

- ✓ Allocation – have all grants received been correctly allocated to the statements of financial position and comprehensive income.
- ✓ Valuation – if a grant may become repayable, a contingent liability may be required.
- ✓ Valuation (initial) – non-monetary grants (e.g. at nominal value (e.g. cost) or fair value).
- ✓ Presentation – clear accounting policy notes.

AUDIT OF FINANCIAL STATEMENTS

Evidence

- ✓ Correspondence with government.
- ✓ Bank statements to confirm receipt.
- ✓ Correspondence with legal advisers and other specialists to confirm:
  - ➤ Eligibility for application for a grant; and
  - ➤ Continuing compliance with the terms of it.

4.5 Discontinued operations

Materiality

- ✓ Highly material information for use by the analyst/broker community and other users.
- ✓ Costs associated with the closure (redundancy, contracts terminated, assets to be sold off, etc) will usually be separately disclosed as, by definition, they are material.

Relevant accounting standards

- ✓ IFRS 5 *Non-current Assets Held for Sale and Discontinued Operations*

Assertions most at risk

- ✓ Completeness – disclosure required when the operation meets the criteria of held for sale or is sold.
- ✓ Presentation – extensive disclosure requirements.

Evidence

- ✓ Minutes of directors/management meetings/co-ordinated plan.
- ✓ That the discontinued operation is separately identifiable.
- ✓ Schedules separating the operating performance of the target segment from the remaining business.

4.6 Impairment of assets

Materiality

- ✓ Impairment usually has material financial impact.

Relevant accounting standards

- ✓ IAS 36 *Impairment of Assets*

Assertions most at risk

- ✓ Completeness – lack of disclosure of events to auditor.
- ✓ Valuation (initial) – future cash flows correctly calculated using appropriate cost of capital.
- ✓ Valuation (subsequent) – correct application of IAS 36 requirements (e.g. for write back for a CGU).

AUDIT OF FINANCIAL STATEMENTS

Evidence

- Details of the event resulting in the impairment.
- Management/directors minutes identifying and quantifying the extent of impairment
- Budgets, forecasts and projections for the remaining useful life of the asset or CGU concerned.
- Detail of recoverable amount as an estimation.
- Calculations of value in use (including evidence on cash flows and cost of capital).
- Formal schedules of impairment review.

4.7 Earnings per share (EPS)

Materiality

- Because of the importance of EPS to investors, the amount is an important disclosure.

Relevant accounting standards

- IAS 33 *Earnings per Share*

Assertions most at risk

- Completeness – number of shares in issue (basic EPS) and potential ordinary shares (diluted).
- Occurrence – changes in share structure.
- Valuation (initial) – measurement of the EPS and diluted EPS.
- Presentation – reluctance to presenting diluted EPS with preference to present "headline" EPS figures to reduce the prominence of IAS 33 required disclosures.

Evidence

- Schedules showing the calculation of basic and diluted EPS, in particular potential shares for diluted EPS.
- Consistency of calculation and measurement. Discussions with management if changes made.
- Statutory returns showing changes in the number of shares in issue during the year.
- Minutes/authorisation of convertible loan stock, convertible preferred shares, options, warrants, etc.
- Disclosures made in accordance with IAS 33.

4.8 Sale and leaseback

Materiality

✓ If land and buildings, will usually be material. There is also a risk that appropriate disclosures will not be made, thus a potentially material qualitative error.

Relevant accounting standards

✓ IAS 17 *Leases*
✓ IAS 24 *Related Party Disclosures* (if sale and leaseback with a related party).

Assertions most at risk

✓ Completeness – that the sale and leaseback is recognised. Finance lease liabilities recognised and correctly calculated. Disclosed in full.

✓ Classification – correctly recognised as a finance or operating lease. Can be difficult if embedded in another transaction (e.g. payment for sole rights to generating capacity).

✓ Valuation and allocation – finance lease asset/liability is correctly calculated (e.g. fair value, rental revenue, finance rate implicit in the lease) and allocations (e.g. depreciation and interest charges) made.

✓ Occurrence, rights and obligations – failure to correctly recognise and present a finance transaction.

Evidence

✓ Board minutes and contracts.
✓ Cash book (e.g. proceeds from sale, rental payments, finance payments).
✓ Risks and rewards of ownership (control).
✓ Confirmation from counterparty on lease terms.
✓ Comparison to market rentals re fair value rent paid.
✓ Recalculation of carrying (fair) values, relevant deferred gains/losses, movements to income statement.

4.9 Share-based payments

Materiality

✓ Impact of expensing share options is, on average, 5% – 10% of net profit after tax (20 – 25% for technology-based entities).
✓ Assumptions and calculations can be complex and extensive disclosures are required.

Relevant accounting standards

✓ IFRS 2 *Share-based Payment*
✓ IAS 19 *Employee Benefits*
✓ IAS 33 *Earnings per Share*

AUDIT OF FINANCIAL STATEMENTS

Assertions most at risk

✓ Classification – may be recognised as:

   ➤ Equity-settled;
   ➤ Cash-settled; or
   ➤ Choice of either.

✓ Classification – because of the complication of many arrangements, transactions may be recognised as a share-based payment, when they are not.

✓ Classification – goods or services received are recognised when obtained.

✓ Valuation – can be complex in absence of market value. All transactions are measured at fair value. A suitable valuation model may need an auditor's expert.

✓ Accuracy – particularly for employee share-based transactions with vesting conditions, the allocation of the expense over the vesting period can cause significant calculation and allocation problems.

✓ Understandability – ensuring that disclosures are relevant, complete, meaningful and understandable can be a significant task. Main disclosures include:

   ➤ nature and extent of arrangements;
   ➤ their valuation; and
   ➤ their impact on the financial statements.

✓ Occurrence – for example, the granting of options, exercise during the year of options, and forfeiture.

Evidence and procedures

✓ For new options granted, directors' approval for employees and shareholder approval for directors.

✓ Obtain deed granting the option and details of performance conditions/period of service and, if appropriate, market conditions.

✓ Numbers of vested employees and options.

✓ Check option valuation. An active market is unlikely, so an appropriate option valuation model should be used. Expert valuation procedures may apply.

✓ Consider deferred tax implications, if relevant.

✓ Assess reasonableness and check mathematical accuracy of projection of expected leavers during vesting period.

✓ Assess probability of achieving market performance conditions and agree to revision of projections.

✓ For options exercised during the year, check to share issue and registration documentation.

✓ Check accounting entries in general ledger: employee/director remuneration and equity.

AUDIT OF FINANCIAL STATEMENTS

- ✓ Directors' remuneration disclosure (if appropriate) verified to ensure options included.
- ✓ EPS: confirm correct number of outstanding options is included in fully-diluted EPS calculation and reperform calculation.

4.10 Financial instruments

Materiality

- ✓ Potentially considerable.
- ✓ Going concern basis – past events have demonstrated the inherent risks of derivatives and other financial instruments to a company's health.

Relevant accounting standards

- ✓ IAS 32 *Financial Instruments: Presentation*
- ✓ IFRS 7 *Financial Instruments: Disclosure*
- ✓ IFRS 9 *Financial Instruments*
- ✓ IFRS 13 *Fair Value measurement*

Assertions most at risk

- ✓ Completeness – failure to present /disclosure an instrument can lead to material misstatement.
- ✓ Completeness/Accuracy – high volumes and complexity of the transactions can make confirming completeness and accuracy very difficult.
- ✓ Completeness/Occurrence – risk of unauthorised transactions, hidden transactions, traders exceeding authority limits, taking excess risks, etc.
- ✓ Valuation – this can be extremely difficult, especially where a previously liquid market becomes illiquid.
- ✓ Disclosure – very complex and detailed and requirements under IFRS undergo frequent revisions. Discursive disclosures include estimation uncertainty, related risks and uncertainties.

4.11 Foreign currency transactions

Materiality

- Where an entity conducts the majority of its business involving foreign currency transactions or has extensive foreign currency denominated loans.

Relevant accounting standards

- IAS 21 *The Effects of Changes in Foreign Exchange Rates*
- IFRS 7 and IFRS 9 deal with most foreign currency derivatives as well as hedge accounting for foreign currency items.

Evidence

- Understanding the financial instruments used by the entity, the risk management and monitoring procedures.
- Assessing the understanding of the financial instruments of senior management and the board.
- Reviewing the approval, recording and tracking process that ensures all financial instruments, hedges and derivatives are completely and accurately recorded.
- Auditor's expert.
- Contracts and counterparty agreements for each instrument.
- Confirmation from counterparties.
- Test fair value where active market exists.
- Test fair value models where used for appropriateness, assertions, assumptions and sensitivity using experts as required.
- Ensure allocation of instruments to category appropriate and that conditions have not been breached.
- Use IFRS 7 checklist.
- Verify risk disclosures (credit, market, liquidity risk etc) to knowledge of the client and its environment.

AUDIT OF FINANCIAL STATEMENTS

Assertions most at risk

- Classification – monetary or non-monetary items, functional currency.
- Valuation – correct exchange rate used on initial recognition and at period end.
- Allocation – exchange differences treated correctly:
  - Monetary items go through profit or loss;
  - Non-monetary at fair value through profit or loss;
  - Non-monetary at fair value through (revaluation) reserves (equity) go through equity (**not** profit or loss).
- Allocation, cut-off – where a period transaction is not settled until after the period end, the total exchange difference is correctly allocated to each period.
- Completeness, classification and understandability – disclosures in accordance with IAS 21.

Evidence and procedures

- Understand control systems for determining foreign currency transactions and conversion into functional currency (and reporting currency, if different).
- Test controls and/or separate transactions to ensure correct exchange rate used.
- Compare any average rate used for profit or loss to actual rate(s) and confirm not materially.
- Confirm functional currency consistent with prior year and economic effects of underlying transactions.
- Agree appropriateness of any change in functional currency.
- Ensure that the transition requirements of IAS 21 have been correctly applied.
- Agree that non-monetary items at historic cost are recorded at the historical translated rate of exchange.
- For non-monetary items at fair value agree:
  - translation at period-end exchange rate; and
  - correct treatment of exchange difference.
- Where presentation currency is different to the functional currency, ensure the correct procedures of IAS 21 followed:
  - assets and liabilities translated at the closing rate (including comparatives);
  - income and expenses at actual or average rate;
  - exchange differences recognised in other comprehensive income.

GROUP AUDITS

1 ISA 600

1.1 Definitions

- "Group engagement partner" – auditor with the responsibility for reporting on group financial statements.

- "Component auditor" – an auditor who, at the request of the group engagement team, performs work on financial information related to a component of the group.

- "Component" – an entity or business activity whose financial information is included in the group financial statements.

- "Significant component" – A component identified by the group engagement team that is:
  (i) of financial significance to the group; or
  (ii) likely to include significant risks of material misstatement of the group financial statements (due to its specific nature or circumstances).

1.2 Group engagement partner

- Responsibilities are the same as for an individual company but with a group aspects (e.g. group structure, group wide controls and consolidation process).

- Must determine whether sufficient appropriate audit evidence can reasonably be expected to be obtained in relation to the consolidation process and the financial information of the components. Considerations:

  ➢ materiality of portion of group financial statements being audited;

  ➢ knowledge of the business of the components (i.e. the whole group);

  ➢ risk of material misstatements in the financial statements of components audited by another auditor; and

  ➢ additional procedures on components audited by another auditor.

- Assess the professional competence of the other auditor in the context of the specific assignment.

- Perform procedures to obtain sufficient appropriate audit evidence that the work of the other auditor is adequate for the principal auditor's purposes

- Consider the significant findings of the other auditor.

- Consider the impact of the other auditor's work when reporting on the group financial statements.

1201

©2015 DeVry/Becker Educational Development Corp. All rights reserved.

- If the other auditor qualifies his opinion, consider the impact of that qualification on the group as a whole. If material to the group, then qualify the group opinion accordingly.

- If component is material to the group and the principal auditor concludes that the work of the other auditor cannot be relied upon and sufficient alternative work cannot be carried out, the principal auditor should express a qualified opinion (limitation of scope).

2 SPECIFIC APPROACH

2.1 Component auditors

- Is similar to using any member of staff.

- Obtain an understanding of the companies audited by the other auditor(s). Consider the overall risk and materiality (of each company and its components) to the group as a whole.

- For all material group companies, obtain the client's permission to contact the other auditors.

- Assess the professional codes of ethics and behaviour followed by the other auditors (e.g. ACCA, IFAC or equivalent). If inappropriate discuss with holding company's management and consider impact on reliance on other auditor's work and group audit report.

- Consider matters such as integrity, objectivity, independence (from group), confidentiality, conflicts of interest, recruitment, training, professional qualifications and CPD. If inappropriate, as above.

- Review audit methodologies, technical manuals and working papers used by other auditor. If inappropriate, consider use of own systems/tailored programmes (provided other auditor competent to use).

- Planning considerations for group as a whole:

  ▲ Changes in group structure – effective date, audit arrangements, accounting policies adopted, auditing standards used by auditors, non-coterminous year ends.

  ▲ Inter-company transactions (trading, non-current assets, management charges, dividends, loans, other), unrealised profits on such transactions, inter-company balances.

  ▲ Transactions between group companies.

  ▲ Inter-company guarantees and security (e.g. bank loans guarantees, rights of set-off, pledged assets). These will need to be disclosed.

  ▲ Group accounting instructions.

GROUP AUDITS

- Plan with/review audit plan (strategy and work programme) of other auditors. The principal auditor must be satisfied that all matters required to form a group opinion have been included (e.g. specific risks, inter-company transactions, group accounting policies).

- Ensure other auditors report any potential problems as soon as they arise so that the group audit plan can be re-assessed as necessary (i.e. supervision).

- Review other auditors' working papers to confirm that appropriate auditing standards have been applied and their work can be relied on in reaching a group opinion. (Including the management letter and contentious issues or matters for manager/partner attention.)

- Review completed consolidation questionnaire (similar to review checklist) covering matters requested at the planning stage and closedown documentation.

- Consolidation questionnaire may be sufficient without a detailed review of the working papers (e.g. if other auditor is part of the principal auditor's network and applies exactly the same procedures).

- Carry out a group subsequent events review. Signing the group audit report may be some time after the completion of the other auditor's work (due to preparing the consolidation) it will be necessary for the other auditors to conduct this review on their clients.

Going concern

- Review on basis of the group as a whole.

- Where some group companies are dependent on the support of their parent, obtain a letter of support ("comfort letter") confirming that parent (or another subsidiary) is willing and able to support.

- Confirmation should be audited (e.g. approved by board of parent, parent's financial strength and cash flows support their assertion of support).

2.2 Consolidation audit work

- Audit procedures include evaluating:

  ▲ whether all components have been included in the consolidated financial statements;

  ▲ the appropriateness, completeness and accuracy of consolidation process and adjustments and reclassifications; and

  ▲ whether any fraud risk factors or indicators of possible management bias exist.

1203

GROUP AUDITS

Consolidation schedule

- ✓ Assess design and implementation of controls over its preparation and test key controls (e.g. mathematical accuracy of the model/programme used).
- ✓ Agree all subsidiaries are included (none excluded unless control lost).
- ✓ Cast and cross-cast all consolidation schedules.
- ✓ Agree opening balances and permanent consolidation adjustments to prior year and consolidation audit working papers.
- ✓ Agree amounts to audited component financial statements and/or audited consolidation returns.
- ✓ Reperform sums.
- ✓ Agree approach is consistent with prior year.
- ✓ Agree accounting policies consistently applied from prior year.
- ✓ Recalculate any accounting policy adjustments from subsidiary to group basis.
- ✓ Agree correct treatment of any impairment of goodwill.
- ✓ Reconcile movements on reserves and for non-controlling interests.

Additions in year

- ✓ Confirm date of control used by management as appropriate.
- ✓ Recalculate pre-acquisition reserves and post-acquisition revenue and expenses.
- ✓ Ensure correct treatment of cash flows.
- ✓ Recalculate goodwill on acquisition.
- ✓ Ensure that each balance of the acquisition is correctly included in the consolidation.
- ✓ Ensure appropriate treatment of dividends paid/declared by subsidiary.
- ✓ Agree (if a listed group) the impact on segmental reporting.
- ✓ Agree correct reason and treatment of entity if not consolidated.

GROUP AUDITS

Disposals in year

- ✓ Confirm date of the loss of control.
- ✓ Agree sales proceeds to sales contracts and other supporting records (e.g. cash books).
- ✓ Agree correct treatment of any deferred or contingent sales proceeds, including fair value calculations.
- ✓ Recalculate profit or loss on disposal and confirm the correct treatment in the group financial statements.
- ✓ Agree correct treatment (disposal of an investment) in the individual financial statements of the parent, including taxation issues. Reconcile profit or loss on disposal to the group figure.
- ✓ Agree that results up to the date of disposal have been correctly treated, including cash flows.
- ✓ Confirm that all assets (including goodwill) and liabilities are removed on consolidation.
- ✓ Consider if the disposal should be treated as a discontinued operation.
- ✓ Agree correct accounting treatment if disposal does not result in loss of control or remaining interest is an associate or joint venture.

Statement of cash flows

- ✓ Agree make up of group statement of cash flow to the supporting financial statements of the group.
- ✓ Agree to audited group returns that inter-company cash flows have been correctly identified and eliminated.
- ✓ Agree correct treatment of cash flows relating to non-controlling interests and associates.
- ✓ Confirm correct cash flow treatment of subsidiary net assets, purchase/disposal of subsidiary and cash impact on acquisition or disposal.
- ✓ Agree to management and working documents, cash flow disclosures relating to the purchase/disposal of subsidiaries.

Reporting date, year end

- ✓ If a subsidiary has a non-coterminous reporting date discuss with management why this is still appropriate.
- ✓ If the entity has prepared additional financial information to enable it to be consolidated at the group reporting date, agree that this information has been correctly incorporated.
- ✓ If no additional information has been prepared, agree that the reporting date is within 3 months of the group reporting date and obtain confirmation that no material matters have arisen that need to be taken account of.

GROUP AUDITS

Foreign translation

- ✓ Agree accounting and disclosure requirements of IAS 21 applied.
- ✓ Test check that assets and liabilities translated into the presentation currency at the closing exchange rate.
- ✓ Test check that income and expenses translated at actual rates.
- ✓ Where average rate used for profit or loss, agree that this rate is acceptable compared to actual rates throughout the year.
- ✓ Agree reconciliation of opening equity foreign exchange reserve to closing balance for both the parent and non-controlling interest (through other comprehensive income).
- ✓ Ensure goodwill is treated as an asset in the financial statements of the subsidiary with related exchange rate difference accounted for in other comprehensive income.
- ✓ If a foreign subsidiary has been disposed of, ensure related exchange reserve is reclassified through profit or loss. If a partial disposal, agree inclusion of only the proportionate amount in profit or loss.
- ✓ Agree that foreign associates are similarly accounted for.

3 DEVELOPING COUNTRIES

Potential audit problems

- ✓ Constraints on access to accounting information provided to the auditors.
- ✓ Non-compliance with certain IFRSs may be significant.
- ✓ Language issues may arise (e.g. if IFRS terms do not translate).
- ✓ External confirmations may be less readily available if the infrastructure is underdeveloped and communications are hindered. The banking system may be relatively inflexible in meeting the auditor's needs.
- ✓ Specialist accounting personnel may be lacking. Experts and professional advisors may not be readily available (to provide audit evidence).
- ✓ International firms may be required to set up a joint practice with a local firm in order to be licensed. Local audit staff may lack experience and training in more sophisticated auditing techniques.
- ✓ Systems of controls may be relatively weaker than in developed countries (e.g. without internal audit function, audit committee, etc).
- ✓ Risks in developing countries include: environmental, financial, legal, taxation, ethical, intellectual property, security, managerial logistics and human resources.

ASSURANCE SERVICES

1 ASSURANCE SERVICES

1.1 Overview

✓ Independent professional services that improve the quality of information, or its context, for decision makers and intended to provide high or moderate levels of assurance.

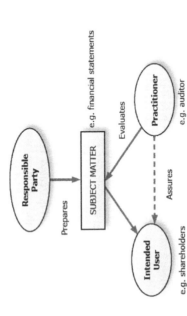

✓ The professional accountant evaluates or measures a subject matter that is the responsibility of another party against identified suitable criteria, and expresses a conclusion that provides the intended user with a level of assurance about that subject matter.

1.1 The professional accountant

✓ Must be a member of an IFAC member body and hence the IESBA Code of Ethics applies.

✓ Must ensure that the pre-conditions for an assurance engagement are relevant.

1.2 Subject matter

✓ May take many forms, for example:

  ▲ Data (e.g. historical, prospective, statistical, performance indicators);

  ▲ Systems and processes (e.g. internal controls, recruitment, quality control);

  ▲ Behaviour (e.g. corporate governance, compliance with regulations, ethics).

✓ Must be identifiable, capable of consistent evaluation or measurement (against the suitable criteria) and in a form that can be subjected to procedures for gathering evidence (to support the evaluation or measurement).

ASSURANCE SERVICES

- ✓ Reasonable level of assurance – engagement risk has been reduced to an acceptably low level for a positive form of expression. (Requires sufficient appropriate evidence to be able to conclude that the subject matter conforms in all material respects with suitable criteria.)

- ✓ Limited level of assurance – sufficient appropriate evidence has been obtained (to be satisfied that the subject matter is plausible in the circumstances) as the basis for a negative form of expression.

1.6 Attestation engagements

- ✓ The conclusion relates to a statement (assertion) made by the responsible party.

- ✓ The professional accountant:
  - ➤ expresses a conclusion about the statement; or
  - ➤ provides a conclusion about the subject matter in a form similar to the statement made.

1.7 Direct reporting engagements

- ✓ The professional accountant expresses an opinion on the subject matter, based on suitable criteria, regardless of whether the responsible party has made a written statement on the subject matter (e.g. compliance with an agreed quality control programme).

1.3 Criteria

- ✓ Standards or benchmarks used to evaluate or measure the subject matter of an assurance engagement.

- ✓ Need to be suitable to enable reasonably consistent evaluation or measurement of the subject matter and must be context sensitive (i.e. relevant to the engagement process).

- ✓ Examples include IFRS for financial statements; internal procedure manual for the operation of that procedure; internal control framework for internal controls; laws and regulations for compliance with such laws or regulations; contract terms and conditions for performance under that contract.

1.4 Engagement process

- ✓ Similar to the audit process – agree terms of engagement, understand business, consider materiality and engagement risk, plan and conduct the engagement to obtain sufficient appropriate evidence and apply professional judgement to be able to express an opinion.

1.5 Conclusion

- ✓ Provides a level of assurance as to whether the subject matter conforms in all material respects with the identified criteria.

ASSURANCE SERVICES

2 REASONABLE ASSURANCE ENGAGEMENTS

Minimum information requirements (ISAE 3000)

- ✓ ISAE 3000 provides specific standards to be applied on reasonable assurance engagements. These are very similar to those for an audit.
- ✓ ISAs are referred to as necessary on assurance engagements (e.g. ISA 500 and ISA 620).
- ✓ Additional elements relevant to understanding the Framework include:
  - ➤ Only accept engagement if the subject matter is identifiable, can be subjected to evidence gather procedures and is the responsibility of another party (e.g. as evidenced by a written acknowledgement, legislation or a contract).
  - ➤ Criteria may be established (e.g. laws and regulations) or specifically developed.
  - ➤ Criteria will be suitable when relevant, reliable, neutral (i.e. free from bias), understandable and complete.

- ✓ Title and addressee.
- ✓ Description of the engagement and identification of the subject matter.
- ✓ The responsible party and description of the practitioner's responsibilities.
- ✓ Where applicable, the parties to whom the report is restricted and for what purpose it was prepared.
- ✓ The standards under which the engagement was conducted.
- ✓ The criteria so readers can understand the basis for the conclusions.
- ✓ Practitioner's conclusion, including any reservations or denial of a conclusion.
- ✓ Report date.
- ✓ Name of firm/practitioner and place of issue of report.
- ✓ Conclusion should clearly express circumstances giving rise to disagreement or limitation of scope.

2.1 Report

- ✓ Should be tailored to the specific engagement circumstances.

Reasonable level assurance report (extracts)

The objective of this Assurance engagement is to report on the effectiveness of the internal control structure for financial reporting of Jasper Inc. The directors of Jasper Inc are responsible for maintaining an effective internal control structure including controls in relation to financial reporting. The directors' assertion about the effectiveness of the internal control structure for financial reporting is included on page 23 of the Jasper Inc 2000 Annual Report.

Our responsibility is to express a conclusion on the effectiveness of the internal control structure for financial reporting to the shareholders of Jasper Inc. This conclusion is based on the procedures that we determined to be necessary for the collection of sufficient appropriate evidence, that evidence being persuasive rather than conclusive in nature, in order to obtain a reasonable level of assurance as to the effectiveness of the internal control structure. Because of the inherent limitations of any internal control structure, errors or irregularities may occur and not be detected. Also, projections of any evaluation of internal control to future periods are subject to the risk that the internal control may become inadequate because of changes in conditions, or that the degree of compliance with the control procedures may deteriorate.

This Assurance engagement has been undertaken in accordance with the International Standard on Assurance Engagements 3000 and accordingly included such tests and procedures, as we considered necessary in the circumstances.

These procedures have been undertaken to determine whether the internal control structure has been adequately designed and operated effectively based on the [Framework] of the Committee of Sponsoring Organisations of the Treadway Commission. Based on our engagement procedures, the inherent limitations outlined above and the evidence collected, we conclude that Jasper Inc maintained, in all material respects, an effective internal control structure in relation to financial reporting for the period .... to .... in accordance with [Framework]

Limited level direct report (extracts)

The objective of this Assurance engagement is to report on the implementation of the Group's national voluntary redundancy program during the period .... to .... The Chief Executive Officers are responsible for the implementation of the program.

ASSURANCE SERVICES

Our responsibility is to express to the Group's Audit Committee a conclusion on whether the voluntary redundancy program has been complied with. This conclusion is based on the application of limited procedures that we determined to be necessary for the collection of sufficient appropriate evidence in order to provide a moderate level of assurance; that evidence being persuasive rather than conclusive in nature.

This Assurance engagement has been undertaken in accordance with the International Standard on Assurance Engagements. This involved the selection of five operating divisions based on the materiality of redundancy expenditure. These divisions represented 67% of the number of redundancies and 73% of the expenditure on redundancy packages during the period ……… to ……… .

Our procedures were restricted to a review of documentary evidence and analytical procedures, and provide less evidence than would be available by applying more extensive and comprehensive procedures. The evidence provided by these procedures to identify the existence, adequacy and implementation of the Group's "Managed Redundancy Program Policy", restricts the assurance to a limited level

It was noted that as a general matter the need for and the benefits arising from redundancies are not well planned or measured, and there is no comparison of the costs of the redundancy program compared to benefits. In the case of the Zt83 Division, the decision to outsource the IT function, resulting in 50 personnel being categorised as surplus to requirements and taking voluntary redundancy, did not meet competitive tendering requirements and was not subject to cost/benefit analysis.

Based on our engagement procedures and the evidence collected, except for the above reservations, nothing has come to our attention that causes us to believe that the voluntary redundancy program has not, in all material respects, been implemented during the period ……… to ……… in accordance with the Group's "Managed Redundancy Program Policy".

ASSURANCE SERVICES

3 RISK ASSESSMENT

✓ Assurance that an entity's profile of business risks is comprehensive and evaluation of whether appropriate systems are in place to effectively manage those risks.

✓ Independent assessments of the likelihood of significant adverse events and possible magnitudes.

✓ Include:

- ➢ identification and assessment of primary potential risks faced by an entity;
- ➢ independent assessment of risks identified by an entity; and
- ➢ evaluation of an entity's systems for identifying and limiting risks.

✓ Evolving into continuous, real-time assurance, thus implying embedded monitoring of systems or direct regular enquiries.

- ➢ Need for pro-active monitoring rather than re-active monitoring.
- ➢ Mind-set must be quality-by-design and continuous improvement rather than inspection-rejection-rework.

4 SYSTEMS QUALITY AND RELIABILITY

✓ Assurance that information systems provide reliable information for operating and financial decisions. Focuses on how well the system fulfils its role.

- ➢ Information integrity and controls.
- ➢ Internal control effectiveness.

4.1 Systems quality

✓ Provides users with assurance that a system has been designed and operated to produce reliable data. Involves testing (continuously) the integrity of an information system.

4.2 Systems reliability

✓ Provides an indication of the quality of information coming out of the organisation's systems over a period of time (evolving to be continuously).

✓ Data from which the information is provided may be internally or externally generated.

✓ Covers both internal (e.g. management corporate governance) and external (e.g. customer or surfer) use of the data store (e.g. database, website) to provide information.

ASSURANCE SERVICES

5 SERVICE ORGANISATIONS

- **Type 1** approach concerns the design and implementation of the control systems. (Should always be available as part of understanding the control system.)
- **Type 2** approach concerns the effectiveness of the control system and is obtained when audit assurance is sought from reliance on control effectiveness of the service provider.

5.1 Materiality

- Relates to system being reported on, not the financial statements.
- Type 1 = qualitative
  Type 2 = qualitative and quantitative
- Although a deviation may not be significant to the service provider, it may be to the service user.

5.2 Evidence for Type 1 report

- Control objectives stated in the service organisation's description of its system are reasonable.
- Identified controls were implemented.
- Risks to control objectives being achieved identified.
- Controls suitably designed to meet objectives and manage risks.

5.3 Evidence for Type 2 report

- Apply standard testing for operating effectiveness, taking into account:
  - performing other procedures in combination with inquiry to obtain evidence about how the control was applied, the consistency with which the control was applied and by whom or by what means the control was applied;
  - controls to be tested depend on other controls (indirect controls) and, if so, whether it is necessary to obtain evidence supporting the operating effectiveness of those indirect controls;
  - the characteristics of the population to be tested (number of controls, frequency of application and the expected rate of deviation); and
  - determining means of selecting items for testing that are effective in meeting the objectives of the procedure (e.g. apply standard sampling approach).

1307

5.4 Written representations

✓ Reaffirm the assertion accompanying the description of the system given by the service organisation;

▲ that it has provided the service auditor with all relevant information and access agreed to; and

▲ that it has disclosed to the service auditor any of the following of which it is aware:

(i) Non-compliance with laws and regulations, fraud, or uncorrected deviations attributable to the service organisation that may affect one or more user entities;
(ii) Design deficiencies in controls;
(iii) Instances where controls have not operated as described; and
(iv) Any events subsequent to the period covered by the service organisation's description of its system up to the date of the service auditor's assurance report that could have a significant effect on the service auditor's assurance report.

5.5 Other information

✓ ISA 720 – the service auditor must read any other information that is contained in a document containing the description of the service organisation's system and the service auditor's assurance report to identify any material inconsistencies with that description

✓ If found, and the service organisation refuses to remove or correct, further actions by the service auditor may take include:

▲ Requesting the service organisation to consult with its legal counsel as to the appropriate course of action;

▲ Describing the material inconsistency or material misstatement of fact in the assurance report;

▲ Withholding the assurance report until the matter is resolved.

▲ Withdrawing from the engagement.

5.6 Subsequent events

✓ Carry out inquiries whether the service organisation is aware of any events subsequent to the period covered by its description of the system up to the date of the assurance report, that could have a significant effect on the assurance report.

ASSURANCE SERVICES

- If the service auditor is aware of such an event, and information about that event is not disclosed, then disclose the information in the assurance report.

- The service auditor has no obligation to perform any procedures regarding the description of the service organisation's system, or the suitability of design or operating effectiveness of controls, after the date of the assurance report.

6 ELECTRONIC COMMERCE

- Assurance that systems and tools used in e-commerce provide appropriate data integrity, security, privacy and reliability.

- Encompasses privacy and security transactions and communications and web assurance.

6.1 Integrity services

- Provide assurance that:
  - the elements of a transaction or document are as agreed among the parties; and
  - the systems that process and store transactions and documents do not alter those elements.

6.2 Security services

- Provide assurance that:
  - parties to transactions and documents are authentic and the transactions and documents are protected from unauthorised disclosure; and
  - the systems that support transaction processing and storage provide appropriate authentication and protection.

7 PUBLIC SECTOR PERFORMANCE INDICATORS

- That part of an economy that provides basic government services.

- Performance measures are based on stakeholder requirements and the relationships between inputs, outputs and outcomes (e.g. value for money).

- A performance audit is an independent examination of efficiency and effectiveness, having regard for economy.

- An audit of performance information aims to assess the relevance and reliability of reported information – data reliability (accurate, complete), quality of content (relevant, comparable, verifiable) and compliance with reporting requirements (timely).

REVIEWS AND RELATED SERVICES

1 OTHER ENGAGEMENTS

1.1 Comparison

Auditing	Other		Compilation
Audit	*Review*	*Agreed upon procedures*	*Compilation*
Reasonable, but not absolute assurance	Limited assurance	No assurance	No assurance
Positive assurance report	Negative assurance report	Factual findings of procedures	Identification of information compiled

1.2 Approach

Is broadly the same regardless of the assignment:

- ✓ Comply with the ethical code (independence only applies to assurance engagements where a reasonable or limited level of assurance is required).
- ✓ Understand the nature of the assignment and the form of report that may be given.
- ✓ Issue an engagement letter.
- ✓ Plan the work carried out.
- ✓ Do the work in accordance with appropriate ISAs.
- ✓ Review the work.
- ✓ Consider subsequent events.
- ✓ Issue the appropriate report/statement.

1.3 Terms of engagement

- ✓ The form of a professional accountant's letter of engagement is basically the same regardless of the service being carried out.

Basic elements

- ✓ Nature and objective of the service being performed.
- ✓ Management's responsibility for subject matter.
- ✓ Scope of assignment work including reference to ISAs.
- ✓ Access to records, documentation and other information requested (or as agreed) for the assignment.
- ✓ A sample of the report expected to be rendered.
- ✓ Statement that the engagement cannot be relied on to disclose errors, illegal acts or other irregularities.
- ✓ Statement that an audit is not being performed and that an audit opinion will not be expressed.
- ✓ Limitation of distribution of report.

REVIEWS AND RELATED SERVICES

1.4 Reports for limited assurance engagements

- Title.
- Addressee.
- Opening or introductory paragraph:
  - reason for engagement;
  - identification of subject matter; and
  - statement of responsibilities.
- Scope paragraph.
- Applicable auditing standards (e.g. ISAs).
- Limitation of work carried out (supports level of assurance provided).
- Audit not performed, procedures provide less assurance than an audit.
- A statement of negative assurance.
- Date of report.
- Auditor's address.
- Auditor's signature.

1.5 Reports where no assurance is given

- Additional elements include:
  - Auditor is not independent of entity (where relevant);
  - Report restricted to parties that have agreed to procedures;
  - Report relates to specific subject matter and not to any other elements;
  - No assurance give – reporting element often a statement of fact;
  - No audit or review (if not a review) carried out; and
  - Had an audit or review been carried out, other matters might have come to light and been reported.

2 REVIEW ENGAGEMENT (ISRE 2400)

- To enable an auditor to state whether, on the basis of procedures which do not provide all the evidence that would be required in an audit, anything has come to the auditor's attention that causes the auditor to believe that the financial statements are not prepared, in all material respects, in accordance with an identified financial reporting framework (negative assurance).

REVIEWS AND RELATED SERVICES

Procedures

- Inquire of persons having responsibility for financial and accounting matters:
  - whether all transactions have been recorded;
  - whether financial statements prepared in accordance with basis of accounting indicated; and
  - any changes in business activities and accounting principles and practices.
- Carry out analytical procedures covering comparison of financial statements with prior periods & anticipated results and financial position, and study of relationships of elements of financial statements that would be expected to conform to a predictable pattern.
- Inquire concerning actions taken at meetings that may affect the financial statements.
- Read financial statements to consider whether they appear to conform with the basis of accounting indicated.
- Obtain reports from other auditors, if any.
- Obtain written management representations when appropriate.
- Inquire about subsequent events.

2.1 Programme of work

Typical "general" tests

- Inquire whether all financial information is recorded completely, promptly and is authorised.
- Inquire about accounting policies and consider whether they comply with IFRS, have been applied appropriately and consistently.
- Inquire about the existence of transactions with related parties, how they have been accounted for and that they have been properly disclosed.
- Inquire about contingencies and commitments.
- Inquire about plans to dispose of major assets and business segments.
- Obtain explanations from management for any unusual fluctuations or inconsistencies in the financial statements.

2.2 Example work programme – trade payables

- Inquire about the accounting policies for initial recording and any entitlement to discounts.
- Obtain and consider explanations of significant variations in account balances from previous periods or from those anticipated.

REVIEWS AND RELATED SERVICES

- ✓ Obtain a schedule of trade payables and determine whether the total agrees with the trial balance.
- ✓ Inquire whether balances are reconciled with suppliers' statements and compare with prior period balances.
- ✓ Consider if material unrecorded liabilities could arise.
- ✓ Inquire whether payables to shareholders, directors and other related parties are separately disclosed.

2.3 Report (extracts)

"We have reviewed the accompanying statement of financial position of …."

"Our responsibility is to issue a report …. based on our review."

"We conducted our review in accordance with …"

"A review is primarily limited to inquiries of company personnel and analytical procedures ….and thus provides less assurance than an audit."

"We have not performed an audit, and accordingly, we do not express an audit opinion."

"Based on our review, nothing has come to our attention that causes us to believe that the accompanying financial statements do not give a true and fair view in accordance with International Accounting Standards"

2.4 Qualified reports (extracts)

Material, but not adverse

"Management has informed us that inventory has been stated at its cost which is in excess of its net realisable value. Management's computation, which we have reviewed, shows that inventory, if valued at the lower of cost and net realisable value as required by International Accounting Standard 2 ….."

"Based on our review, except for the effects of overstatement of inventory described in the previous paragraph, nothing has come to our attention …."

Adverse

"As noted in X, these financial statements do not reflect the consolidation of the financial statements of subsidiary companies …."

"Based on our review, because of the pervasive effect on the financial statements …. The accompanying financial statements do not give a true and fair view …."

3 REVIEW OF INTERIM FINANCIAL STATEMENTS

✓ The objective of the engagement is to conclude whether, on the basis of the analytical procedures applied and inquiries made, anything has come to the auditor's attention that suggests that the information is not prepared in all material respects in accordance with an identified financial reporting framework

3.1 Procedures

✓ Interim financial information will not usually include sufficient information to give a true and fair view. The scope of the review involves less work than a full audit and therefore provides a lower (moderate) level of assurance.

✓ The review work will be broadly similar to that detailed above.

✓ The review will not include:

- tests of accounting records through inspection, observation or confirmation;
- obtaining corroborative evidence in response to enquiries; or
- other typical audit tests (e.g. test of controls or detailed testing of assets and liabilities).

3.2 Going concern

✓ The auditor should consider whether any significant factors identified at the previous audit have changed to such an extent as to affect the appropriateness of the going concern basis.

✓ Particular attention should be given to the period since reporting on the last full financial statements.

✓ Enquiries may be limited to discussions with management about changes to cash flow and banking arrangements where there are no significant concerns.

3.3 Report (extracts)

"We have reviewed the accompanying statement of financial position of ...*(etc)*"

"On the basis of our review we are not aware of any material modifications that should be made to the financial information as presented for the six months ended 30 June 20X5."

REVIEWS AND RELATED SERVICES

4 DUE DILIGENCE

> The process of systematically obtaining and assessing information in order to identify and contain the risks associated with a transaction (e.g. buying a business) to an acceptable level.

> A due diligence review may merely validate information previously obtained. For example:

> - from a set of audited financial statements;
> - a review of tax returns; or
> - an examination of accounting and administrative practices.

> Or it may consider specific non-financial matters (e.g. organisational, business risk, HR or cultural fits).

> The scope of a due diligence assignment usually varies between:

> - a review concentrating on financial and specific operations matters (e.g. inventory control or manufacturing processes); and
> - a comprehensive review on every aspect of the seller's company (financial and non-financial).

> In comparing the audit of receivables, the due diligence work on receivables may be:

> - detailed testing (as for an audit); or
> - a review of debt-aging, collectability, allowances for doubtful debt and bad debt write-offs; or
> - seller representations and warranties (which might introduce "purchase price hold backs").

5 AGREED-UPON PROCEDURES (ISRS 4400)

> Procedures of an audit nature to which the auditor, the entity and any appropriate third parties have agreed and to report on factual findings.

> Standard audit procedures may be used, but as the scope of the work is based on the client's requirements, the work is not an audit.

> No level of assurance is given. The report is based on the factual findings of the auditor. The recipients of the report must draw their own conclusions from the auditor's findings.

5.1 Report (extracts)

> "We have performed the procedures agreed with you and enumerated below with respect to ..... Our engagement was undertaken in accordance with the International Standard on Related Services (ISRS) 4400 .... The procedures were performed solely to assist you in .... and are summarised as follows: ....."
>
> "We report our findings below: ....."
>
> "Because the above procedures do not constitute either an audit or a review ... we do not express any assurance on ...."
>
> "Had we performed additional procedures or had performed an audit or review .... Other matters might have come to our attention that would have been reported to you."
>
> "Our report is solely for the purpose set out in the first paragraph .... and is not to be used for any other purpose or to be distributed to any other parties."

PROSPECTIVE FINANCIAL INFORMATION

1 PROSPECTIVE FINANCIAL INFORMATION (ISAE 3400)

✓ Financial information based on assumptions about events that may occur in the future and possible actions by an entity. Can be in the form of a:

- forecast;
- projection; or
- combination (e.g. a one year forecast plus a five year projection).

✓ Relates to a future period or an expired period where the auditor has yet to report.

1.1 Objectives

✓ To ensure that:

- Assumptions are not unreasonable and consistent with purpose of information;
- PFI is properly prepared on the basis of the assumptions; and
- PFI is properly presented and all material assumptions are adequately disclosed (as best-estimate or hypothetical assumptions).
- PFI is prepared on a consistent basis with historical financial statements, using appropriate accounting principles.

1.2 Accepting the engagement

✓ Consider:

- Form of PFI and its intended use.
- Professional accountant's own competence and experience.
- The business – its economic substance and stability.
- Management's competence, integrity and past record in preparing PFI.
- Whether information will be for general or limited distribution.
- Form of opinion and recipient.
- The nature of assumptions (i.e. best-estimate or hypothetical).
- The elements to be included in the information.
- The period covered by the information.
- Time available.
- The acceptability of any limitations.

✓ Do not accept (or withdraw from) an engagement if the assumptions are clearly unrealistic or the PFI will be inappropriate for its intended use.

PROSPECTIVE FINANCIAL INFORMATION

1.3 Knowledge of the business

- Must be sufficient to evaluate whether all significant assumptions required for the preparation of the PFI have been identified.

Considerations

- Internal controls over preparation of PFI and expertise and experience of persons involved. (Meet management to ascertain how PFI is prepared);
- Nature of documentation supporting management's assumptions;
- Extent to which statistical, mathematical and computer-assisted techniques are used;
- Methods used to develop and apply assumptions;
- Accuracy of PFI prepared in prior periods and reasons for significant variances; and
- Extent of reliance on historical financial information (Audited? Prepared using acceptable accounting principles? Modified reports?).

1.4 Period covered

Considerations

- Operating cycle (e.g. time required to complete a major construction project).
- The degree of reliability of assumptions (e.g. short prospective periods for introducing new products).
- The needs of users (e.g. time required to generate sufficient funds to repay a loan).
- Assumptions become more speculative as the length of the period covered increases.

1.5 Examination procedures

- The likelihood of material misstatement.
- Knowledge obtained during any previous engagements.
- Management's competence in preparing PFI.
- The extent to which PFI is affected by the management's judgment.
- Adequacy and reliability of the underlying data.

PROSPECTIVE FINANCIAL INFORMATION

Procedures

- Assess source and reliability of evidence supporting assumptions;
- Consider significant implications of hypothetical assumptions;
- Make clerical checks such as recomputation;
- Review internal consistency of amounts based on common variables (e.g. interest rates);
- Focus on areas particularly sensitive to variation that will have a material effect on the PFI;
- Consider the interrelationship of other components in the financial statements;
- When any elapsed portion of the current period is included in PFI, consider the extent to which procedures need to be applied to historical information; and
- Obtain written management representations regarding:
  - intended use of PFI;
  - completeness of significant management assumptions; and
  - management's acceptance of responsibility for PFI.

1.6 Presentation and disclosure

- Whether presentation of PFI is informative and not misleading.
- Whether accounting policies are clearly disclosed in the notes to the PFI.
- Sensitivity in material areas.
- Whether assumptions are adequately disclosed.
- The date as of which the PFI was prepared.
- The basis of establishing points in a range.
- Any change in accounting policy since the most recent historical financial statements.

PROSPECTIVE FINANCIAL INFORMATION

1.7 Report format

- ✓ Title.
- ✓ Addressee.
- ✓ Identification of the PFI.
- ✓ A reference to ISAE 3400 (or equivalent).
- ✓ Statement of management's responsibility for PFI.
- ✓ The purpose and/or restricted distribution of the PFI.
- ✓ A statement of negative assurance.
- ✓ A "properly prepared" opinion.
- ✓ Appropriate caveats.
- ✓ Date of report on which procedures completed.
- ✓ Auditor's address.
- ✓ Auditor's signature.

1.8 Modified opinions – examples

- ✓ PFI is inappropriate for intended use ⇒ adverse opinion (or withdraw from the engagement).
- ✓ Significant assumptions appear unrealistic ⇒ adverse (depending on circumstances).
- ✓ Serious lack of information to support reasonableness ⇒ disclaimer (limitation of scope).
- ✓ Omission of information that could be misleading ⇒ adverse (or withdrawal from engagement).
- ✓ Inadequate presentation and disclosure ⇒ qualified (or adverse opinion or withdraw from engagement).

1.9 Report examples

Example 1 – Report on a forecast

We have examined the company's profit forecast covering the twelve months ending on the 30th June 20X7 in accordance with International Standard on Assurance Engagements (ISAE) 3400 *The Examination of Prospective Financial Information*.

Management is responsible for the forecast including the assumptions set out in Note X on which it is based.

Based on our examination of the evidence supporting the assumptions, nothing has come to our attention which causes us to believe that these assumptions do not provide a reasonable basis for the forecast.

Further, in our opinion the forecast is properly prepared on the basis of the assumptions and is presented in accordance with [relevant financial reporting framework].

Actual results are likely to be different from the forecast since anticipated events frequently do not occur as expected and the variation may be material.

PROSPECTIVE FINANCIAL INFORMATION

Example 2 – Report on a projection (extracts)

We have examined the projection of the profits ….. Management is responsible for …..

This projection has been prepared for ………. As the entity is in a start-up phase the projection has been prepared using a set of assumptions that include hypothetical assumptions about future events and management's actions that are not necessarily expected to occur. Consequently, readers are cautioned that this projection may not be appropriate for purposes other than that described above.

Based on our examination of the evidence supporting the assumptions, nothing has come to our attention which causes us to believe that these assumptions do not provide a reasonable basis for the projection, assuming that sales growth of 10% is achieved and costs are contained to a growth rate of 6% per annum.

Further, in our opinion the projection is properly prepared on the basis of the assumptions and is presented in accordance with generally accepted accounting principles.

Even if the events anticipated under the hypothetical assumptions described above occur, actual results are still likely to be different from the projection since other anticipated events frequently do not occur as expected and the variation may be material.

FORENSIC AUDITING

1 FORENSIC AUDITING

1.1 Definitions

- *Forensic accounting* – engagements that result from actual or anticipated disputes or litigation.

- *Forensic audit* – The process of gathering, analysing and reporting on data, in a pre-defined context, for the purpose of finding facts and/or evidence in the context of financial/legal disputes and/or irregularities and giving preventative advice in this area

1.2 Forms

Fraud investigation (corruption, asset misappropriation and financial statement fraud)

- Prove or disprove suspicions.
- Identify the individuals involved.
- Identify motive, opportunity and rationale.
- Quantify losses.
- Provide the evidence for appropriate criminal proceedings.
- Identify risks of fraud and advice on managing the risks to an acceptable level.

Negligence

- Personal injury, fatal accident, medical negligence, professional negligence, personal negligence in causing damage to other's property
- Identify circumstances and impact
- Establish financial compensation required (e.g. for loss of earnings through injury).

Insurance claims

- Establishing loss of profits due to business interruption.
- Investigating and establishing quantity and value of a destroyed asset (e.g. inventory in a fire).

Other

- Contract, copyright, royalty and matrimonial disputes.
- Asset tracing (e.g. money laundering and proceeds of crime).

1.3 Approach

- Broadly the same approach as to any assurance engagement under ISAE 3000 as many auditing techniques will be used during the investigation.

- Ethics, quality control, engagement, planning, obtaining evidence and reporting.

- Integrity and objectivity must be of the highest order.

- The risks of self-review, advocacy and management threats to objectivity must be managed to ensure an acceptably low level.

- Competence covers legal, auditing, investigative, interview, interrogation, personal skills and court proceedings (including acting as an expert witness under cross-examination).

- The scope of the investigation, objectives, management's responsibilities, use of assumptions, estimates and judgement, form and content of the final report, timescale of investigations and report, access to information and people must all be established and encapsulated in an engagement letter.

- The report will be of a factual nature and is unlikely to provide any assurance (e.g. a true and fair view).

AUDITOR REPORTS

1 BASIC PRINCIPLES

- Audit objectives:
  - to form an opinion; and
  - express it in a written report.

Considerations

- Sufficient appropriate evidence obtained.
- Uncorrected misstatements are not material.
- Prepared in accordance with financial reporting framework (e.g. IFRS).
- Adequate disclosure of significant accounting policies.
- Accounting policies are consistent with the financial reporting framework and statutory requirements.
- Accounting estimates are reasonable.
- Information presented is relevant, reliable, comparable and understandable.
- Adequate disclosure of all material matters.
- Terminology used is appropriate.
- "Fair presentation" achieved.

1.1 Basic elements (ISA 700)

- Addressee.
- Opening or introductory paragraph.
- Statements of responsibility.
- Scope paragraph.
- Opinion paragraph.
- Date of audit completion.*
- Auditor's address.
- Auditor's signature and name.

* **Never** before approval of financial statements.

1.2 Modified reports

- Emphasis of matter.
- Other matter.
- Modified opinion.

1.3 Modified opinions

- Qualified "except for".
- Adverse.
- Disclaimer of opinion.

2 UNMODIFIED REPORT

INDEPENDENT AUDITOR'S REPORT TO …

We have audited … [financial statements].

Management's Responsibility for the Financial Statements

… for the preparation and fair presentation of these financial statements in accordance with [financial reporting framework] and internal control … [preparation of financial statements that are free from material misstatement, whether due to fraud or error].

Auditor's Responsibility

… to express an opinion on these financial statements based on our audit. We conducted our audit in accordance with … Those standards require that we comply with ethical requirements and plan and perform the audit to obtain reasonable assurance whether the financial statements are free from material misstatement.

An audit involves … [description].

We believe that the audit evidence we have obtained is sufficient and appropriate to provide a basis for our audit opinion.

Opinion

In our opinion, the financial statements present fairly [or give a true and fair view] of the financial position of [Company] as of [date] and of its financial performance and its cash flows for the year then ended in accordance with …

Name and signature
Date
Address

3 EMPHASIS OF MATTER AND OTHER MATTER PARAGRAPH

3.1 Distinction

✓ To draw users' attention to:
  ➤ A matter that is fundamental to understanding the financial statements; or
  ➤ Any other matter that is relevant to understanding.

Emphasis of matter

✓ Immediately after Auditor's Opinion.

✓ Headed "Emphasis of Matter".

✓ Clear reference to matter emphasised and where relevant disclosures can be found.

✓ Indicate that audit opinion is **not** modified in respect of this matter.

Other matter

✓ Immediately after Auditor's Opinion and any Emphasis of Matter paragraph.

✓ Headed "Other Matter".

✓ State clearly that other matter is not required to be presented and disclosed in the financial statements.

✓ Do not include matters prohibited by law or required to be given by management.

3.2 Circumstances when used

Emphasis of matter

- ✓ Material matter regarding a going concern problem.
- ✓ Significant uncertainty.
- ✓ Early application of a new accounting standard.
- ✓ A major catastrophe that has had, or continues to have, a significant effect on the entity's financial position.

In our opinion ... [as for unmodified opinion]

Emphasis of matter

Without qualifying our opinion we draw attention to Note X to the financial statements ... [description].

Other matter paragraph

- ✓ Material matter that does not affect financial statements (e.g. material inconsistency in other information).
- ✓ Where the auditor wishes to withdraw from an engagement but cannot do so because of law.
- ✓ To elaborate on matters that provide further explanation of the auditor's responsibilities.

In our opinion .... [etc.]

Other matter

As required by s267 of the Companies Act 20X0, we confirm that there are no other matters, as defined by s266, concerning our audit to be reported.

4 MODIFIED OPINION

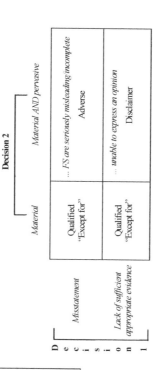

- ✓ If *misstatement* basis of opinion should include:
  - ▸ a clear description of the reasons; and
  - ▸ quantification of possible effects, when practicable.

AUDITOR REPORTS

✓ If *lack of sufficient appropriate evidence*:
  - describe limitation; and
  - indicate possible adjustments.

4.1 Sample standard opinions

Lack of sufficient appropriate evidence – qualified opinion

> We have audited ... Management is responsible for ... Our responsibility ... [all standard wording].
>
> *Basis for Qualified Opinion*
>
> [Description of items in financial statements affected, including amounts]
>
> We were unable to obtain sufficient appropriate audit evidence about ... [amounts described above] because [reason]. Consequently, we were unable to determine whether any adjustments to these amounts were necessary.
>
> *Qualified Opinion*
>
> In our opinion, **except for** the possible effects of the matter described in the Basis for Qualified Opinion paragraph, the financial statements present fairly, in all material respects, ...

Pervasive lack of sufficient appropriate evidence – disclaimer of opinion

> We were engaged to audit the accompanying financial statements .... *(no change to remaining words)*
>
> *Management's Responsibility ... (no change to wording)*
>
> *Auditor's Responsibility*
>
> Our responsibility is to express an opinion on these financial statements based on conducting the audit in accordance with International Standards on Auditing. Because of the matters described in the Basis for Disclaimer of Opinion paragraph, however, we were not able to obtain sufficient appropriate audit evidence to provide a basis for an audit opinion.
>
> *Basis for Disclaimer of Opinion*
>
> [Description of circumstances]
>
> *Disclaimer of Opinion*
>
> **Because of the significance** of the matters described in the Basis for Disclaimer of Opinion paragraph, we have not been able to obtain sufficient appropriate audit evidence to provide a basis for an audit opinion. Accordingly, we do not express an opinion on the financial statements."

AUDITOR REPORTS

Materially misleading – qualified opinion

> We have audited ... Management is responsible for .... Our responsibility is to express an opinion *(no change)*
>
> *Basis for Qualified Opinion*
>
> [Description of items in financial statements affected, including amounts]
>
> *Qualified Opinion*
>
> In our opinion, **except for** the effects of the matter described in the Basis for Qualified Opinion paragraph, the financial statements present fairly, in all material respects ....

Materially misleading and pervasive – adverse opinion

> We have audited ... Management is responsible for .... Our responsibility is to express an opinion ....
>
> *Basis for Adverse Opinion*
>
> [Description]
>
> *Adverse Opinion*
>
> In our opinion, **because of the significance** of the matter discussed in the Basis for Adverse Opinion paragraph, the financial statements do **not** present fairly ....

ADDITIONAL READING

ARTICLES

The following technical articles written by members of the P7/auditing examining team can be found on the ACCA website at:

http://www.accaglobal.com/ubcs/en/student/exam-support-resources/professional-exams-study-resources/p7/technical-articles.html

It is essential that articles written by the examining team are read and understood. Always access the ACCA P7 website for new articles published before the exam.

Exam technique

- Examiner's approach update (March 2013)
- Continue to be rest assured (Jan 2013)
- Exam technique for P7 (May 2012)
- How to tackle audit and assurance case study questions Part 2 (Nov 2009)
- Exam technique (Sept 2009)
- The importance of financial reporting standards to the auditor (Apr 2009)
- How to tackle audit and assurance case study questions Part 2 (Sept 2007)
- How to tackle audit and assurance case study questions Part 1 (Aug 2007)

ADDITIONAL READING

Topic specific

- Laws and regulations
- Audit quality – a perpetual current issue
- Professional scepticism
- Using the work of internal auditors (Sept 2014)
- Staying on the right side of ethics (Sept 2014)
- Accounting issues (Sept 2014)
- Forensic accounting (Sept 2014)
- IAASB developments (May 2014)
- Reporting on audited financial statements (Nov 2013)
- Internal controls of companies (June 2013)
- A question of ethics (Nov 2012)
- Planning an audit (Oct 2012)
- Completing the audit (Oct 2011)
- Group audits (Apr 2011)

WEBSITES

The higher skills required for Professional papers include analysis, interpretation, commercial awareness and professional commentary. Your ability to enhance these skills will be greatly improved by regular research of key websites.

Websites to be considered as "favourites" include:

- ACCAglobal.com
- IFAC.org (International Federation of Accountants)
- Accountancyage.com (Accountancy Age)

EXAMINER'S REPORT – JUNE 2015

This is a summary of the main points. The full report can be found at: http://www.accaglobal.com/en/student/acca-qual-student-journey/qual-resource/acca-qualification/p7/examiners-reports.html

General Comments

The performance of candidates continues to be extremely mixed.

At this sitting there were some excellent scripts which clearly demonstrated a thorough understanding of the syllabus content, and displayed effective application and analytical skills.

However, performance overall continues to be disappointing.

Many of the weaker scripts indicated that candidates had limited knowledge of auditing principles and that candidates struggled to appropriately apply knowledge to the question scenarios.

A number of common issues arose in candidates' answers that contributed to the disappointing pass rate:

✗ Writing too little for the marks available – this was especially the case for Q1(c), Q3 (b), and Q4(c).

✗ Providing answer points that were not relevant to the requirement – in particular for Q1 (a), Q3 (b) and Q3(c).

✗ Failing to discuss, explain or generally expand on points beyond simple identification of facts given in the question.

✗ Answers often lacked the detailed evaluation and assessment that is required at this level.

✗ Writing points that were much too vague and failing to display either technical knowledge or application skills.

✗ Illegible handwriting and poor presentation.

✗ Lack of knowledge on certain syllabus areas.

✗ Lack of basic accounting knowledge – for example not understanding debits and credits or whether accounting errors would lead to the overstatement or understatement of balances and transactions.

Section A

Question One (35 marks)

Set in the planning phase of the audit of a new audit client. The company had experienced significant growth in recent years, and had become listed in its home jurisdiction during the financial year.

Information was provided on the company's financial background, its operations and corporate governance structure.

Part (a) "discuss the matters specific to an initial audit engagement which should be considered in developing the audit strategy" (6 marks).

✓ The best answers concentrated on practical matters relevant to the requirement.

✗ Weak candidates provided generic answers (wrote learnt checklist) irrelevant to the requirement.

✗ Other weak answers discussed general audit planning matters that were not tailored to the specifics of this scenario.

! Answer the specific question requirement that has been set.

✗ It was not relevant to discuss whether the audit firm should take on the client and associated acceptance issues as it was clearly expressed in the scenario that this decision had already been taken and consequently answers of this nature scored limited credit.

! Read, understand and apply the detail from the scenario.

Part (b) "Evaluate the audit risks to be considered in planning the audit" (17 marks)

✓ Excellent answers covered a range of audit risks, all well explained, all relevant to the scenario and demonstrated that a methodical approach, clearly working through the information logically, had been applied to the information in the scenario.

✓ Strong candidates attempted to prioritise the various risks identified thus demonstrating appropriate judgment and an understanding that the audit partner would want to know about the most significant risks first (professional approach).

! This is the approach that should be used for all P7 questions.

EXAMINER'S REPORT – JUNE 2015

Common mistakes:

- ✗ Discussing business risks (**not asked for**) instead of audit risks
- ✗ Spending time explaining the components of the audit risk model (**not asked for**)
- ✗ Including answer points that were too vague to be awarded credit.
- ✗ Incorrect comments on accounting treatments.
- ✗ Lack of knowledge on accounting issues.
- ✗ Evaluation of the company's corporate governance structure, but not linking this to audit risk.
- ✗ Incorrect materiality calculations.
- ✗ Some candidates tried to make the recommended procedures much too complicated, not appreciating that traded equity shares can be easily valued and documented.

! Lack of commercial understanding.

- ✗ The procedures in relation to EPS were often very vague.
- ✗ Very few candidates noted that the weighted average number of shares would need to be verified given that the company had a share issue during the year.

! Lack of IFRS understanding resulting in poor audit procedures.

Professional marks (4)

- ✗ Presentation was not always good and candidates are reminded to pay attention to determining an appropriate layout for their answer.

Part (c) "Recommend audit procedures to be performed on the portfolio of short term investments and on the EPS figure" (8 marks)

- ✓ Some candidates proved able to provide a good list of recommendations.
- ✗ Most candidates could only provide vague suggestions.

EXAMINER'S REPORT – JUNE 2015

Question Two (25 marks)

Part (a) "Comment on the matters to be considered and explain the audit evidence you would expect to find in a review of the working papers" (16 marks).

The first issue related to a sale and leaseback arrangement.

✓ Answers on the whole were good.

The second issue related to the acquisition of a 52% shareholding in a company, which had been accounted for as an associate in the consolidated financial statements.

✓ Most candidates were able to identify that the accounting treatment seemed incorrect and could explain their reasoning.

✗ Fewer candidates appreciated the impact of the loss-making status of the company acquired.

✓ Most candidates could provide some evidence points, with the most commonly cited being the board approval of the acquisition and agreeing the cash paid to bank statements.

✗ Fewer candidates could suggest how the audit firm should obtain evidence on the exercise of control by the parent company or on the mechanics of the consolidation that should have taken place.

Part (b) "Discuss the implications of the impact of breaches of laws and regulations on the completion of the group audit" (9 marks)

✓ Most candidates identified the obvious issues.

✓ The best answers used a methodical approach to explain the auditor's responsibilities in relation to a suspected breach of laws and regulations.

✗ Weaker answers focussed solely only on one issue.

✗ Weaker answers simply stated facts without much attempt to apply the requirements of ISA 250 *Consideration of Laws and Regulations in an Audit of Financial Statements*, to the scenario.

✗ Some candidates demonstrated a lack of judgment or real understanding of the role of the auditor in relation to laws and regulations.

Question Three (20 marks)

It was quite clear that many candidates had chosen to attempt this option question because they had read the relevant article on professional scepticism, but that they had very limited knowledge on either impairment audit issues or on forensic investigation procedures.

EXAMINER'S REPORT – JUNE 2015

! **Poor exam technique. Only select a question on the basis that there is a good chance of obtaining a strong pass mark.**

Part (a) "Explain the meaning of the term professional scepticism and to discuss its importance in planning and performing an audit" (5 marks).

✓ It was clear that many candidates had read and understood the contents of a recent article on the topic of professional scepticism.

✓ Most answers provided an appropriate definition of professional scepticism and went on to discuss how it links to audit quality.

✗ Few candidates discussed the recent activities of the regulatory bodies in respect of professional scepticism.

! **The article made references to further reading that appears to have been ignored.**

Part (b) "Discuss how professional scepticism should be applied to the scenario" (6 marks) and "Explain the principal audit procedures to be performed on the impairment of goodwill" (5 marks).

✓ Many candidates were able to explain that the Group finance director was intimidating the audit firm, that his workings were not sufficient as a source of evidence, and that he may have something to hide.

✗ The requirement relating to procedures on goodwill impairment was poorly attempted. Many candidates did not answer the question, and simply described the accounting treatment for goodwill.

! **Hoping saying something, anything, would gain marks. It will not.**

Part (c) "Recommend the procedures to be used in performing a forensic investigation" (4 marks)

✗ Answers to this requirement were weak.

! **Clear gap in knowledge.**

Question Four (20 marks)

This question was broadly themed around audit quality and ethical issues and featured a company audit for which the audit report on the most recent financial statements had just been issued.

EXAMINER'S REPORT – JUNE 2015

The question was split into three short scenarios, with the requirement to comment on the quality control, ethical and professional issues contained in each with respect to the audit and the firm-wide policies of the audit firm.

Candidates were also required to recommend any actions to be taken by the audit firm.

Part (a) dealt with fee pressure, impact on the audit strategy and quality control (6 marks).

✓ Many candidates attempted this part of the question well.

✓ Effective answers explained the intimidation threat to objectivity caused by fee pressure and went on to discuss the impact of each of the issues raised in the scenario on the quality of the audit that had been performed.

✓ It was pleasing to see many candidates discuss matters such as sampling risk and the need for review procedures to assure the quality of audit work and to reduce the audit firm's detection risk.

✗ Weaker answers tended to be repetitive without adding value. Just saying "not enough evidence could be obtained" was insufficient.

Part (b) focussed on the issue of off-shoring audit work, which had been discussed in an article (5 marks).

Answers ranged in quality, with some good attempts.

✗ Weaker answers tended to suggest that overseas offices would be incompetent and unable to perform even the simplest of audit procedures.

✗ Some candidates misinterpreted the information provided and assumed that the scenario was about using component auditors in a group situation, which was not the case.

Part (c) dealt with the issues of a senior client director joining the audit firm and cross-selling non-audit services (9 marks).

✓ Most candidates realised that there was an ethical threat concerning the new partner, but did not develop the point further

✓ Stronger candidates were able to clearly explain the specific ethical threats that arose from the scenario, provided sensible recommendations, and also commented on the audit firm needing stronger firm-wide policies in the event of recruiting new audit partners from audit clients.

✗ Many candidates failed to deal with the issue of cross selling, concentrating instead on the ethical problems of providing non-audit services to audit clients.

- ✗ A significant number of candidates failed to allocate appropriate time to this part of the question (9 marks) in that their answer was the same length as for part (a) (6 marks).

  the impact for the audit opinion itself and not the overall impact on the audit report, failing to mention the need for a Basis of Opinion paragraph in the audit report.

- ✗ Only the strongest candidates realised that this incorrect accounting treatment may have been applied to other contracts and that opening balances may be incorrect given that this was a new audit client.

Part (b) provided information on a completed contract in respect of which the company was facing legal action due to problems that had arisen following completion of the contract. (6 marks)

- ✓ Candidates seemed confident of the accounting rules.
- ✗ Most candidates failed to identify the potential going concern threat.
- ✗ Most candidates failed to discuss further actions, other than a generic suggestion to "discuss with management".

Question Five (20 marks)

This question dealt with three issues at the completion stage of the audit of a new client. For each issue candidates were required to discuss the implication for the completion of the audit and for the auditor's report, and to recommend further actions to be taken.

- ✓ Generally the question was well attempted by many candidates who seemed well prepared for a question of this type.
- ✗ The main weakness in answers was a lack of specificity in the actions that had been recommended, and in many answers no actions were provided at all, severely limiting the marks that could be awarded.

Part (a) dealt with 100% profit recognition on a long-term contract that was only part completed at the year end (8 marks).

- ✓ Candidates performed well on this requirement.
- ✗ Some candidates missed out on marks by not recommending any further actions or by only discussing

Part (c) dealt with a key performance indicator included in an integrated report (6 marks).

- ✗ A significant minority of candidates were unable to work out a simple percentage increase despite the information being clearly presented in the question scenario.

- ✓ The best answers explained that management should be asked to amend the figure in the integrated report, and that if it remained uncorrected it would not impact on the audit opinion, but should lead to the inclusion of an Other Matter paragraph in the audit report.

- ✗ Weaker answers suggested that the opinion should be modified due to material misstatement.

- ✗ There were few suggestions of further action to be taken other than "discuss with management".

ANALYSIS OF PAST EXAMINATIONS

Topic	Dec 2011	June 2012	Dec 2012	June 2013	Dec 2013	June 2014	Dec 2014	June 2015
Ethics	Q2	Q1/Q4	Q1/Q3	Q1/Q2	Q4	Q4	Q1/Q4	Q4
Professional liability				Q4				
Money laundering		Q3				Q2		
Auditor appointment, tendering		Q1	Q3				Q4	
Professional scepticism		Q3						Q3
Business risk		Q1	Q1				Q1	
Risk of material misstatement		Q1	Q1		Q1		Q1	
Audit risk	Q1			Q1		Q1		Q1
Analytical procedures	Q1							
Group/joint audit		Q1	Q2	Q2/Q5	Q1	Q1	Q2	Q2/Q3
Quality control	Q1	Q3		Q2			Q4	Q4
Due diligence					Q2			
Forensic investigations & fraud	Q4		Q1/Q4	Q2				Q3
PFI, forecasts		Q2			Q5	Q2		
Work of an expert, internal audit	Q3				Q1/Q3			

ANALYSIS OF PAST EXAMINATIONS

Topic	Dec 2011	June 2012	Dec 2012	June 2013	Dec 2013	June 2014	Dec 2014	June 2015
Fraud, Laws and regulations					Q3			Q2
Revenue (recognition, receivables)		Q1	Q4					
Grants		Q1						
Financial instruments				Q4				
Share-based payments	Q1							
Accounting estimates	Q3							
Provisions and liabilities	Q2/Q3				Q3			
Inventory	Q2		Q4					
Non-current assets, leases, intangibles	Q1/Q2	Q5		Q3	Q3	Q3	Q1/Q3	Q2
Earnings per share								Q1
Going concern					Q3/Q5			
Environmental and social performance		Q2					Q3	
Audit completion			Q2			Q3	Q2/Q5	Q5
Auditor's report	Q5	Q5	Q5	Q5	Q5	Q5	Q5	Q5

EXAMINATION TECHNIQUE

TECHNIQUE IN AUDITING QUESTIONS

(1) Understand the requirements

- Before attempting any question, and in order to impress the markers, you need to understand the examiner's requirements.

Read the requirement

- Always read the requirements (at the end of the question) first, never the "scenario". This will put the scenario into context and reduce the risk of answering the question you wanted to see (often enforced if you read the scenario first) rather than the question **set** by the examiner.

Highlight "Instruction" and "Content"

- Nearly all requirements (and parts thereof) have an "instruction" (e.g. "describe") and "content" (e.g. "procedures").

- The instructions tell you how your answer should be written; the content tells you what you should be writing about, for example:

Instructions

- "Describe" (i.e. set out the characteristics of). Use brief sentences but give more depth than if the instruction was "state" (see below).

- "Explain" (i.e. make plain, clarify, elucidate). For example, defining a term does not explain it, but providing an illustration may do so.

- "State" (i.e. express in words). Use one short sentence (bullet point) to make each answer point.

- "Discuss" (i.e. give balanced views on and conclude, where appropriate).

- "List" (i.e. make a list of like things).

- "Justify" (i.e. give reasoning).

- "Identify" (e.g. from the scenario). This requirement is often implied rather than expressly stated. For example, "Describe the risks …." requires that the risks be identified before they can be described.

- "Comment" (i.e. make observations, appraise and/or critically examine).

- "Suggest" (i.e. propose or put forward).

EXAMINATION TECHNIQUE

Content

- "Procedures" and "Work" (may be preceded by the word "audit") – what you should do – requires actions. For example, **A**nalyse, **E**nquire, **I**nspect, **O**bserve and comp**U**te (mnemonic: "AEIOU"). Do not be constrained by such ideas lists at P7 level – think of similar and related actions (e.g. review, ask, confirm, circularise, compare, calculate, etc).

- "Matters", "Factors" (also "Issues" and "Considerations") are things to be taken account of – which must therefore be of relevance (note that they are not "Procedures"). In the context of a planning question these might include risks (see below), materiality, reliance on internal controls, timescale, etc.

- "Internal controls" (or "controls" or "internal control procedures") – what the entity (**not** the external auditor) should be doing to prevent things going wrong.

- Remember that this covers the control environment (e.g. audit committee, organisational structure, management supervision, internal audit and segregation of duties) and the control procedures (e.g. authorisation, control accounts, controlling documents, limiting physical access).

- "Evidence" (i.e. what you want to know, as auditor). To generate ideas think about:

    - sources of evidence (i.e. internal, external, written, oral, auditor-generated)

    - the procedures by which they are obtained ("AEIOU" above); and

    - the financial statement assertions about which evidence is sought – completeness, occurrence measurement, presentation and disclosure, appropriate carrying amount, rights and obligations existence.

- "Implications", "Effect", "Impact" and "Consequences" (i.e. what difference, if any, does it make?)

- "Risks" e.g. of misstatement in the financial statements (from an *auditing* perspective) or of failure of a business objective (e.g. due to unavailable e-commerce systems, credit facilities not renewed).

- "Why" and "Reasons" call for justification. Think "because …" or "due to ….".

- "Enquiries" (i.e. questions). Begin, for example, with "What", "How", "Why" and end with a "?"

2102

©2015 DeVry/Becker Educational Development Corp. All rights reserved.

EXAMINATION TECHNIQUE

- ✓ "Objectives" (e.g. of controls). For ideas consider "CAVe" – **C**ompleteness, **A**ccuracy and **V**alidity (of transactions) and **E**xistence (of resulting assets and liabilities). One way of addressing objectives is to respond "To ensure that ... good things happen (or bad things do not happen)".

- ✓ "Weaknesses", "Limitations" "Disadvantages" etc. Respond with "negative" words like "no", "poor", "difficult". Similarly for "Advantages", "Benefits" etc use "positive" words like "good", "easy". (2) Read the scenario

- ✓ Appreciate the following:

  - ▲ Your "role" in the scenario (e.g. as senior, manager, reporting partner – gives an indication of authority and decision making capabilities).

  - ▲ The dates involved (e.g. the year end, reporting deadline, current date, etc). Paper P7 is set in "real time" – so if you are sitting an exam in December and planning an audit for the year ending 31 December – that is imminent and you will not have yet attended the inventory count.

  - ▲ The "status" of the client (e.g. new or existing; large or small; likely to have an internal audit department).

  - ▲ The nature of the client's business. If relevant, this will give you an insight into the potential factors and problems which you will be required to discuss.

  - ▲ For example, a heavy industrial engineering business is likely to have complex inventory and work in progress while a travel agent would have minimal inventory but would require a system to deal with advance bookings, the taking of deposits and the calculation of commission.

  - ▲ The extent to which the client operates a computerised system, which will affect the tone and jargon of your answer to a question concerning, for example, internal controls.

- ✓ Taking a few minutes to read, highlight and annotate the scenario to pick up such points should be time well-spent.

(3) **Plan your answer**

- ✓ The importance of adequate planning cannot be over-emphasised.

- ✓ Adequate planning leads to an organised logical structure to your answer, incorporating all the points you can come up with and highlighting your powers of analysis and communication.

2103

EXAMINATION TECHNIQUE

- A lack of planning leads to a disorganised illogical jumble of scraps of thoughts and ideas, causing you to omit key elements of the question and repeat answer points already made.

- **Never** write "½ sentences" in a plan – there is no *time* for them in answer planning and no *place* for them in writing out your answer.

- How much planning is needed on each question depends, in the main, on just two factors:

    (i) How much the requirement and scenario are **broken down into parts** – the more detailed this is in the question, the less you need to do.

    (ii) The **mark allocation**. In general, the more marks the more planning will be required.

- When you are practiced in exam technique, planning many questions should take only five minutes.

- Ensure that you read the question thoroughly, as discussed above. Highlight key points or note them down to ensure that you incorporate them in your answer.

- Plan your answer in whatever way you prefer, but at least plan.

- If you jot down an answer plan do so on your answer script, rather than your question paper, so you can submit it. Clearly head up the page "answer plan" or "workings".

(4) Write the answer

- Use underlined <u>HEADINGS</u> and <u>subheadings</u> (generated by the requirement and any breakdown of the scenario into parts) to produce a logical and structured answer.

- This approach is effective in providing focus for your answer and enhances presentation.

- The examiner positively discourages rewording of requirements into introductory sentences because it wastes valuable time and does not earn marks.

- Maintain a sentence structure and keep sentences and paragraphs short and succinct.

- Explain and define where necessary (e.g. if writing to a layman, explain phrases such as "inherent risk" briefly: "inherent risk, that is the susceptibility of an item in the accounts to misstatement …").

- Try to achieve a good standard of English. Note that although you will not lose marks for spelling mistakes and poor grammar, you may lose marks if your answer points cannot be understood by the marker.

EXAMINATION TECHNIQUE

✓ Allow plenty of space to present your answer and, if your writing is difficult to read, write on every other line.

WARNING: Restrict the use of underlining to headings and sub-headings (and use a ruler). Do **not** waste time underlining what you consider to be the "key" words – it is quite unnecessary and may interfere with the marking process. Only use black or blue ink. Do **not** use any other colour. Do **not** use any highlighter, regardless of the colour!

(5) Practise

✓ When attempting an exam style and standard question, *always* practise exam technique so that it is second nature to you by the time of the real exam.

✓ Spend time thoroughly reviewing your answer against the "model" answer and make a note of the points you missed. (Do not be despondent if some of the answers you encounter do not follow this guidance – historically "model" answers are written solely to convey technical content rather than exam technique.

✓ Study the examiner's comments on candidates' performance in previous exams, areas of weakness and suggestions for improvements.

Summary

✓ Remember the key elements to examination technique:

Read: first the requirements to put the scenario into context, then the main body to provide the facts to trigger your knowledge.

Think: without this planning process you will not be able to convey the higher level skills of comprehension, application and analysis.

Write: concentrate on your style of writing to address the examiners' requirements as directly as possible, answer the Q set and think about the ***relevance*** of what you are writing. If it does not add value, why write it?

✓ A trusted answer approach, in the context of this article, has always been: point, explain example. For every point made, explain why it has been made and then give examples for support.

For example "Obtain management representations …" has no meaning in P7 unless you state the representation required, the context it is required in and why it is required.

FREQUENTLY ASKED QUESTIONS

1) Q: Do I really need to go back to Paper P2 and revise all the IFRSs again?

   A: YES – no escape. The audit approach to IFRS is now highly examinable, as made clear by the examiner's article

   An often repeated comment by the examiner in her reports is the poor understanding of IFRS and basic accounting principles by a significant number of candidates. It's as if F7/P2 are in distant memory never to be visited again!

2) Q: As I have passed Paper F8 all I need do is to learn the new bits of the P7 syllabus (e.g. group audits, assurance services etc). Right?

   A: Wrong! Professional papers test a higher set of skills than those required for F8 (e.g. in-depth comprehension, analysis, interpretation, evaluation, judgement, application of theory to practice, inferences, commercial awareness, professional commentary, thinking "outside of the box" etc). You must be able to demonstrate the use of these skills when dealing with the assumed in-depth knowledge of Papers F7, F8 and P2.

   Again, the examiner often comments on the absence of these higher level skills in candidates' answers. Many candidates fail to provide the necessary depth of understanding, analysis and professional comment and just answer the question as if it were from Paper F8.

3) Q: As I am an auditor, surely there is no need to do that much studying?

   A: Do not be lulled into a false sense of security. Whilst your day-to-day work provides excellent practical experience in some areas of the syllabus it is unlikely that your range of work will cover all the areas that will be examined in sufficient depth, (e.g. professional appointments, assurance services, current issues).

   Study system application and external research are essential.

FREQUENTLY ASKED QUESTIONS

4) Q: Are the Study System and question banks sufficient to get me through? If I learn everything in the study system, will I learn enough to pass?

A: The Study System and question banks are as a comprehensive a set of material that you will be able to find.

However, you must supplement your studies by reading all relevant Student Accountant articles and reviewing appropriate websites (e.g. ACCA, IFAC, IASB) and the financial press (e.g. Financial Times, Economist) to keep yourself abreast of current developments.

Very few marks will be gained just by rote learning the study system or articles in Student Accountant.

The key is to be able to apply the underlying theory and knowledge learnt from the study system, together with your practical experience and research, to the practical environment demanded by the exam.

Past P7 question practice is critical to be able to understand how the examiner thinks and works.

5) Q: How critical are the articles in Student Accountant written by the examiner?

A: Very! Examiners, in general, are very busy people. They will therefore only write articles with a purpose (i.e. the subject is very likely to be examined at some stage in the future).

Note that the Exam Notes state that whilst topics of EDs are examinable, a detailed knowledge of the EDs will only be examined to the extent that relevant articles are published in Student Accountant. So if you do not read these articles